"True Brit"

The Adventures of Peter Fidler of Bolsover: 1769–1822

By
K. Gordon Jackson

COUNTRY BOOKS

Published by Country Books
Courtyard Cottage, Little Longstone, Bakewell, Derbyshire DE45 1NN England

British Library Cataloguing-in-Publication Data
A CIP catalogue record for this book is available from the British Library

ISBN 1 898941 48 3

Printed in Great Britain

Dedicated to

Mrs Mary Fidler of Bolsover, who
kept alight Peter Fidler's forgotten
adventures for over 30 years
and
to **Bridgidt Bowers-Jackson** who had
the unenviable task of listening to me
when I was excited and she was tired.
and
to the **ordinary people of Bolsover,**
Derbyshire, England, who, unbeknown to most
of them, already had a hero.

K.Gordon Jackson
August 1999

Illustrations

Permission to use the following material has been given, courtesy of the Provincial Archives of Manitoba & Manitoba Museum(Hudson's Bay Company Archives) which hold the copyright. **(a) to (h)**

(a) Hunting a Buffalo Bull (Painting by George Catlin for the Hudson's Bay Company)

(b) Trading Ceremony at York Factory, Hudson's Bay 1780. (Painting by Adam Sheriff Scott RCA)

(c) Philip Turnor and Peter Fidler 1791 (Painting by Lorne Bouchard for the Hudson's Bay Company)

(d) Portage along Lake Athabaska.

(e) A Buffalo Jump

(f) Loading Up With Supplies at a Trading Centre

(g) Plains Indians Weapons.

(h) Strip Surveys at Red River by Peter Fidler

(i) Peter Fidler. 32 ft statue carved from Redwood Tree

(j) Fidler's birthplace: Sutton Mill Farm, Bolsover, England. Rear view

(k) Fidler's birthplace: Sutton Mill Farm, Bolsover England. Front view.

(l) Ault Hucknall Church, Derbyshire, England.

(m) Bolsover Castle. Engraving 1695

(n) Cumberland House, Trading Post.

(o) List of Native Canadian Tribes

(p) Cairn to the Memory of Peter Fidler, Dauphin, Manitoba, Canada, Courtesy of the Fort Dauphin Museum.

Foreword

"True Brit" This book is designed to raise awareness of Peter Fidler, Explorer, Surveyor and Fur Trader in the area where he was born. However, it is not meant to be definitive. It charts the chronological events of Peter Fidler's life, very loosely in Derbyshire, England although more tightly in Rupert's Land. Details of Peter's childhood are veiled, other than date and place of birth, baptism etc., but, he certainly received a broad-based education. My own deductions lead me to believe that he attended The Grange School at Hardwick Hall, Derbyshire, followed by Netherthorpe Grammar School, both of which were within range of his home. The precise reason for leaving home and travelling to Cheapside, London, is not clear. It would be very far, expensive and alien for a 16 year old boy from the country. Nevertheless, that's where he had been living for two years when he 'signed-up' as a labourer with the Hudson's Bay Company in 1788. Unless, perhaps, he had travelled at someone else's expense, say, as a companion or servant, to St. Paul's School in London, a common enough practice for educated working-class boys.

Explorers Captain Cook and Captain Vancouver, Alexander Mackenzie and Samuel Hearne are some of the men who determined the broad outlines of the Canadian northwest. But they left behind huge empty voids to be explored by others.

The great surveyor-geographers and traders who fulfilled that gigantic and dangerous task were Philip Turnor, David Thompson and Peter Fidler who between them mapped almost all the unknown western interior. Others travelled it, but few had the ability to record it. Turnor opened up the interior from Hudson Bay. He trained Thompson and Fidler who, in turn, continued the task into the western plains, forests, prairies and to the Rocky Mountains. Thompson wrote a book entitled Narrative' which was acquired and edited by J B Tyrrell.

Fidler wrote no book, but his records are contained in his surveying journals which show him to be Thompson's equal.

In the new settlement of Chesterfield House at the junction of the Red Deer and South Saskatchewan Rivers, Fidler drew a map in February 1902 with the assistance of a Blackfoot Chief named 'The Feathers' (Ac Ko Mo Ki). It showed huge parts of the continent unknown to Europeans and encompassed the 'Mis is oury' River, the Rockies, the coastal belt, and it identified hitherto unknown tribes.

Fidler submitted it with his work on 23rd October 1802 to Alexander Lean, Secretary of the Hudson's Bay Company. By 17th December, it was sent by Lean to Sir Joseph Banks, President of the Royal Society and to Alexander Dalrymple, Hydrographer to the Admiralty. The papers were deposited with Aaron Arrowsmith and considered so important that they were published by that world-renowned London cartographer. The maps showed the drainage system of the Missouri River from the Rocky Mountains and were used by President Jefferson of the USA as a future route for expanding the American empire to the Pacific Northwest. They were passed to and used by the American Lewis and Clark expedition in 1804.

Fidler was the first European to record the Athabascan Tar Lakes, the Coal Seams of Dium Heller, Canadian Cactus, Buffalo jumps, the aftermath of smallpox and measles, tribal war among the Indians and a wide range of other matters that he found interesting. It was imperative to his trading enterprise that he speak Indian languages, understand customs, religions, behaviour, practices etc. He was attacked by gunmen, beaten, starved, his trading posts burned down, raided by indians, but he persevered. Such matters he recorded in his journals. He never forgot his roots and named Forts and Trading houses after places in Derbyshire. Records, written in his own hand are deposited in the Manitoba Museum~Hudson's Bay Archives, Winnipeg.

As the result of his union with Mary, a Cree Indian, whom he married, several hundreds of their descendants live in Canada and Northern USA. Many were surprised to find that their common ancestor was an Englishman from a place called Bolsover, in Derbyshire, England. Even more surprising, citizens of Bolsover, England don't realise that they produced such a hero. Perhaps this book will go some way towards correcting that. The house where he was born still exists, as does the house he built for his mother.

I have taken 'writers liberty' and given Peter a voice. Whether or not he would have said things in the way I suggest, is open to discussion. But he wrote most of them, so I imagine he could have said them too. The same argument applies to Turnor, Graham, and the others.

I am deeply indebted to the Manitoba Heritage Museum (Hudson's Bay Archives) for their help, courtesy and erudition. Almost all of the images are from that source and I acknowledge gratefully their invaluable contribution. Similarly, I am grateful for the scholarship of Dr James G. MacGregor whose book 'Peter Fidler: Canada's Forgotten Explorer' was a great inspiration.

September l 999
K.Gordon Jackson,
Glapwell, Nr Bolsover, Derbyshire.

Contents

Trading ceremony at York Factory in the 1780's

The arrival of the main body of Indians in the early summer was one of the important events of the year at the Hudson's Bay posts.

Their chief can be seen in the 5th row back, walking with the Govermor and smoking a pipe.

(Painting by Adam Sheriff Scott R.C.A. for the Hudson's Bay Compnay.)

CHAPTER 1

'To The Edge Of Wilderness'

Peter Fidler gazed around in bewilderment. The town of York Factory in Hudson's Bay was throbbing with activity. It happened every time a Company ship arrived from England, carrying newcomers, stores, some luxuries and a vast range of goods used for trading with Indians. The bustle and noises were much different than those at sea during the past weeks. More pronounced. Boys chattered, men shouted and laughed gruffly, oars rattled, the Bay ran chuckling up the pebbled beach, carts squeaked, drums beat a tattoo. He recognised a multitude of individual sounds, which, put together, seemed like pandemonium.

Working parties of sturdy young apprentices and labourers formed into regulated lines to unload the ship. Ferries of ships' boats, supplemented by local boats, rowed backwards and forwards from ship to shore emptying the vessel of its contents.

Hunting the buffalo on the prairies

(Painting by George Catlin.)

14

The ship's Captain had been the first to land and pay his respects to the Governor, as was the custom. Now, the Governor attended by red-coated soldiers, an Indian Chief and other dignitaries was drummed and piped on board to collect Company instructions and personal mail carried in the vessel's safe.

Clutching a flat, wooden box under one arm, and with a roll of possessions slung across his back, Peter stepped carefully over the bow of the cutter into cold, shallow water. There was no room to disembark at the jetty.

"Step lively there lad" bawled the Coxswain, eager to get back to his ship through the jostling crowd of small boats.

A small wave pushed against the side of the clinker-built boat, swivelling it sideways. The Coxswain growled in annoyance and barked an order. Oars jutted out and the boat straightened, nose to land.

"Are ye clear, lad?" shouted the Coxswain.

Peter was paddling the last few feet, water just below his knees. He waved a hand in acknowledgement and heard a shout of "Good luck, boy!"

"Are you Fisher, lad?"

Peter was addressed by a man in leather, sleeveless waistcoat and tight leather breeches.

"Fisher sir? No sir. I'm Fidler, sir"

"Fidler? Fidler? Of course you are. Can't imagine why I said Fisher. Well, welcome to the Wild North West, Master Fidler."

He spat a wad of dark brown into the advancing waves and stepped back delicately.

"Filthy habit" he grunted and held out a hand. "I'm Phillip Turnor, Surveyor and you are to be one of my labourers I understand. Walk with me over to that building and I'll find out more about you. Get your legs dried, too. What's your first name?"

"Peter, sir".

Turnor was a head taller than Peter and his stride was half a yard longer. The boy had to trot to keep up.

"What do you have in the box, Peter?"

"It's my writing gear, sir. Quills, ink, some paper, quill sharpener, blotting sand. That sort of thing."

Turnor stopped.

"Mean to tell me that you read and write?"

"Yes sir. And mathematicise and the same for geometry. "

15

"Well, well! Do you now! Talk about Providence!"

He stood with one hand under his chin, deep in thought, oblivious to the goings on around him.

"Right!" he said suddenly and began to walk.

"I've changed my mind about you being a labourer. We need a Writer. Ours has recently died of some unnamed local disease, poor devil. I'll take you on for a couple of months and see how you fare. If you are alright, I'll arrange for you to be put on the Company's books in that capacity. Does that suit you?"

Peter stared round-eyed at the back of Turnor retreating head.

"That's fine with me sir. Very fine". He picked up the rhythm of step and followed Turnor into the long wooden house.

A Company Decision
London, England.

The gavel cracked on to its mahogany pad. All conversation around the table ceased. London fog swirled against the heavily draped windows.

"This Extraordinary meeting of the Honorable Hudson's Bay Company is now in session."

The portly Chairman with hooded eyes looked swiftly around the table.

"I'm going to find it demmed difficult to see some of you through that demmed cigar smoke, so I'll be grateful if you'll forgo them for a while!"

There was a surreptitious shuffling and several footmen in the background proffered deep ashtrays.

"There is only the one subject on this agenda, as I know we are all aware. It concerns the activities of those demmed North Wester scoundrels and the so-called free traders"

"I calls 'em a collection of traitors and poachers!" bawled an irate voice.

Numbers of heads nodded in agreement.

"Don't shout out if you have something to say" snapped the Chairman "else we shall be all talking and nobody listening."

He sat back and laid down the gavel.

"I hear what you are saying and have a great sympathy with your feelings. However, shouting and threatening ain't going to help us to solve the problem. We have a guest with us, gentlemen, as you will have noticed. I think some of you know him, but I shall introduce him nevertheless! He is Mr Phillip Turnor, our very experienced Surveyor from Rupert's Land. I hope to gain your

16

approval to appoint Mr Turnor to help us with our problems"

He turned to the tall, slim man sitting quietly by his right hand side, at the end of the boardroom table.

"I have requested Mr Turnor to give a resume of those problems and make recommendations to deal with them. Unless any Honorable Member has anything to say, may I please invite Mr Turnor to speak"

"What's his background, Chairman. Is he a Gentleman?"

Th[...]ded eyes at the speaker.

[...]udent at the Grey Coats school, sir.

[...]like, but so far as we are concerned"

[...]eting " he is a Gentleman and a long

[...] he was 18 years. Does that answer

[...]veral hard looks from supporters of

[...]r a clearing of throats and movement

[...]; city or town clothes. His colours

[...]legant and fitting a tall, slim body.

[...]op, he began.

[...]light Southern English inflection.

[...]ve been invited here today to share

[...]airman and I have already had a long

[...]mainly in agreement. The wars with the French cost the Company dear, especially the loss of York House, your principal trading settlement on the Hudson's Bay, on two separate occasions. We have it back, of course, but a lot of damage was done, both to material things and to confidence with our erstwhile Indian traders."

Everyone present noticed the change in pronoun from 'your' to 'we' and 'our'.

A wall sized map, of the Northern Territories, once known as Rupert's Land, filled one side of the room opposite large windows. The Chairman gestured to several footmen, who lit lamps and held them for members to see the map's details. Those with their backs to the map, shuffled their chairs around. The Eastern part of the map, contained many names, rivers, lakes, but the centre, NorthWest and West were devoid of detail.

Turnor smiled at a member three chairs away and asked "May I borrow your cane, sir?"

Taking the proffered cane, he pointed to the North West.

"The North West Company has moved from South to North here. They have learned lessons from the French and with their help they are cutting our lines with those Indians who traded with us during the past hundred and fifty years."

Moving his pointer to the centre, he went on.

"NorthWesters and freelance traders are also beginning to operate from the great plains of the South up to the North, They cut our lines of communication even closer to us and we are losing input from the Cree nation and their neighbours, the Chippewyans."

He turned back to the table, picked up a sheaf of papers and riffled them.

"I'm sure that you are familiar with the contents of this year's report. Shareholders will be aware that the Company's profits, whilst sitting at 10 percent, have dropped during the past three years."

He looked around at their faces.

After a few seconds he said

"A continuation of that dividend cannot be guaranteed if the trend continues, gentlemen".

A sudden undercurrent of conversation started then stopped.

"But how do we stop it" a voice blurted and then became silent.

Turnor looked in the direction of the caller, who was busily fussing with a jacket button, face down.

"The Company has had, and still does have, some of the finest traders and explorers to be found anywhere in the world. I'm sure that you will agree?"

Most nodded.

"Mister William Tomison has carried the Company banner for a long time. He is a splendid servant to the Company, a great, stubborn, honest, cross-grained, sterling Orkneyman. The kind of employee worth a king's ransom. And the same kind of description fits his colleague, Mr Robert Longmore. What's more, they have lived with the Indians, speak their languages, and in turn are admired by them. There is only one problem. They have memories of their travels, but no maps."

He stopped and sipped at a glass of water.

"No-one else can follow them" he went on. "So, what we are proposing is that we send traders who are Surveyors and have the language, to remedy the shortage of maps. Part of their remit will be to discover fresh routes along the Churchill River, the Saskatchewan and many others. There are likely to be some 60, 000 miles of riverways to be charted and recorded."

He looked around again.

"It will not be done in five minutes. But we are talking of a Company which has survived disasters for 150 years, and this is part of the preparations necessary, I submit, for the next 150 years."

He stopped.

"Thank you for listening to me. If you have any questions, please feel free to ask them."

He smiled.

"There is no hidden agenda" he said.

A number of hands shot up around the table.

"Demmed civilised today!" said the Chairman. "Yes, Sir George?"

"Turnor speaks very cogently, Chairman, but he's not a shareholder. Not yet anyway!"

Guffaws of laughter greeted him.

"What I would like to know is, where do we find Surveyors? Hey? Where do we find them? They don't grow on trees".

He sat back, pleased at further guffaws.

"A good question, Sir George. I'm sure Mr Turnor has an answer."

"Yes sir. My answer is fairly simple. On site at Hudson's Bay we have a number of apprentices acting as Writers or temporary Assistants to traders. We can recruit others who have all been well educated, such that they are familiar with mathematics, astronomy, geometry and have already proven themselves on site in the territory. Whilst it is not entirely relevant, I may say that several of them have been sponsored by your good selves. They will be our trainees. I shall train them myself.".

The Chairman raised an eyebrow in the direction of Sir George, who remained silent and nodded.

No more questions were forthcoming.

"Very well, Gentlemen. I took the liberty of anticipating your decision and drafted a missive. It shall be read out to you."

He beckoned to a small dark man in a dark suit who appeared almost magically from behinds the Chairman's chair.

"Read it out, Brooklea".

19

Brooklea, cleared his throat and commenced.

"Aaaaaa from the Honourable Hudson's Bay Company to Mr Humphrey Martin, Chief of the Company's York House Factory.

The Bearer, Mr Philip Turnor, being by the Governor, Deputy Governor and Committee of the Honourable Hudson's Bay Company appointed their Surveyor for settling Latitudes, Longitudes, Courses and distances at the different settlements inland.

You are to give the said Gentleman all requisite and possible assistance to enable him to give all satisfaction in the above, or any other duties required of him.

He is to be treated in the most respectful manner and accommodated with every thing requisite to facilitate his Expedition .

On this Account, the Expense it will Occasion must be only Your secondary Object. The Gentlemen, being desirous to have the earliest intelligence of Mr Turnor's proceedings, You will transmit to Us whatever He shall think worthy of their attention.

Signed etc., etc., dated 3rd May 1778"

Brooklea vanished as quickly as he had appeared.

Members crowded around Turnor to wish him luck.

."When shall you be leaving sir?" asked a tall, thin Gentleman

"As soon as I can gather my accoutrements together, sir. Although, I expect to be in York Factory by October".

He smiled at each well-wisher in turn and was led away by the Chairman

Arrival of David Thompson

Weather was changing.

A long, hot summer had turned into an Autumn of reds, yellows and golds.

Indians and French trappers around the post predicted it would soon be winter. A hard one, they repeated, glumly.

The door in front of Peter opened abruptly. A buffalo hide filled the doorway and he jumped up in alarm. The hide fell to the floor, disclosing a young man, slightly older than himself but of similar size. His grin was infectious beneath a thatch of badly cut fair hair.

"Oh God!" said the visitor looking round, "Is this it? Is this where we work?"

The room, even with several lamps burning, was not bright.

20

He groaned loudly, clutched his chest and fell in an exaggerated swoon upon the buffalo hide.

Peter, at a loss what to do, stepped forward, but reared back as the lad rolled over and sat cross-legged.

"I guess that you must be Fidler? It's Peter, isn't it?" he thrust out a hand, and Peter felt that it was firm, hard-skinned and strong.

"I'm David Thompson. You can call me David! I've come to join you".

"Have you? Join me? You mean, helping with the Writing? That'll be very handy."

The youth was easy to like. He jumped up athletically, bundled up the skin and pushed it into a corner.

"I'll have to sleep there until I'm sorted, I suppose. Where are you living?"

"In the opposite corner, over there" said Peter, nodding in that direction. "We don't eat in here, of course. We go to the mess hall just behind this cabin. Except the Indians and Frenchies of course. They prefer their own company"

Thompson laughed.

"Right!" he said, sitting on a rough hewn bench beyond Peter's desk. "Know what you mean. Just spent a winter with the Piegans." He pronounced it 'pee-ey-gans'.

He looked around the sparsely furnished office with a blank expression.

"Don't suppose you'll be upset to leave this place, will you!"

"Leave it?". Peter didn't understand the question.

Thompson looked at him sharply.

"Don't tell me that you haven't been told yet! Oh no! And I've opened my big mouth. Sorry Peter. I suppose I'd better tell you all, but I'd prefer that you act dumb when they tell you. Can you do that?"

"I guess so, but it depends what it is!"

"OK. Mr Turnor has had words about the two of us with the Chief, Mr Tomison. It seems as though our Directors feel there is a need for more Company Surveyors. You and I are to be trained so that we can become Assistants and accompany whoever the Principal Surveyor happens to be. At the moment, of course, it's Mr Turnor, but there may be others. And we'll be there, on the trail, to help them out! I've done a spell at Churchill factory on the Bay, and been to Manchester House Trading post. I've just come back from there and I can tell you, it's hard work, but much more

21

exciting than being at Grey Coat School! I even enjoyed clerking for Mitchell Oman at South Branch House. That's where my boss was George Hudson, you'll have heard of him? He went to Grey Coats and left before I joined.

He chortled gleefully.

"So what do you think of the proposal then, my young bucko?"

Peter was dazed by the Thompson's stories.

"But who is going to do this job, then?" he said lamely.

"For heavens sake, it'll be us, both of us until we finish training. Then somebody else can take it over. I've just been out for the past three weeks with a party headed by Mr Turnor. I wouldn't like to think that I'd be stuck indoors for the rest of my life, however important it may be"

He stood up, excited.

"You haven't been out yet, have you? No. I know you haven't, but you'll love it. There are millions of miles that haven't been seen yet, Indian tribes that have never seen a white man, and Indians that white men have never seen. Things and places to be discovered."

He sat down suddenly..

"Oh God! The thought of working at York Factory until then is enough to drive a man crazy." He groaned.

His quicksilver manner changed and he looked around.

"Where do we wash up for dinner?" he asked, smiling once again.

"Follow me, O Great Buffalo Hunter!"

"I guess you haven't seen a live buffalo yet, have you " said David as they went through a small door at the back of the cabin

"Anyway, how did you come to be here?"

Peter remembered.

Young Fidler Fights The Foe

Howling savages chased him through tall, meadow grass, bordered by ancient hedges and Derbyshire stone walls.

The steep field, swept upwards..

Peter stopped running.

Panting for breath he struggled into his shoes.

The savages stayed in the long grass but fine fronds swayed where they hid.

He took a broad-brimmed, brown hat from inside his jerkin, smoothed

22

it out, jammed it on his head defiantly then waved a baton of rolled documents to ward them off.

The savages remained hidden.

Beyond them, fields and trees drifted down into Scarsdale Valley. To show that he was not afraid, he turned his back on the pursuers and ran towards a hole in the hedge.

It was one that he had used numerous times to escape them and gain access to the lane which ran upwards to his right.

Ault Hucknall church at the hill's summit was his destination. Behind the hedge and other hedges, the intricate silhouetted battlements of Hardwick Hall rose into the sky.

Before the concealed the enemy could pounce, he thrust his way bodily through the narrow opening where he would be free, on neutral ground and they were not allowed to follow.

He bounced back from the haunches of a very large horse, and sat down with a thump. The rolled documents dropped from his hand.

"Well bless my buttons, boy! What on earth are you up to, hey?"

A tall, elegant man in polished riding boots emerged from the far side of the horse. He wore no hat and his greying hair was pulled into a queue on his neck. A white frilled shirt was open at his tanned neck.

Peter, winded, stumbled to his feet. The hat slewed sideways and he snatched it off.

"Sorry, sir. Didn't see you or rather, your horse, just there."

"Didn't see us! Didn't see us! Ain't we not big enough? Ain't we not big enough for you? Hey?"

The horseman had moved to Peter's side of the horse and grasped its bit close to the animal's mouth. It fretted and moved its feet, but remained quiet.

"What the deuce were you playing at, hey? Frightened the life out of Caesar! Yes, frightened the life! You ran as though a thousand devils were after you! What?"

Peter couldn't tell whether the piercing grey eyes were angry or not. He decided to take no chances.

"I really am very sorry, sir. I don't know what came over me. P'raps 'cos I'm a bit later than usual for my lessons". His explanation came to a halt.

"Where the devil have you come from, lad?"

"From Sutton Mill Farm, sir. Bolsover sir. The Miller, Mr Fidler is my father. My name is Peter Fidler sir."

"Well, we've got that bit sorted, ain't we. So you're James' son, are you. And where were you going before my horse and I were trampled underfoot at your sudden appearance?"

"Up there sir," said Peter with a jerk of his head towards Saint John the Baptist church. " We attend church first sir".

He looked down at his shoes.

"I think I'm going to be late, sir. The Schoolmaster, and the Reverend will be at the gate. May I go now, please?"

"So you're a pupil at Hardwick School, hey! Did you run all the way from Bolsover, lad?"

Peter moved uneasily from one foot to the other.

"Yessir. I do it three times a week".

He looked up at the horseman.

"But I hope to move to Netherthorpe school next term".

"That's probably four-and-a-half miles, eight or nine miles each day. Probably more along the bottom of the Dale."

His Lordship seemed to be musing to himself.

Then he said loudly

"You can go lad and tell the Reverend and Mr Derrey that Scarsdale held you up and that's why you're late. Got it? Hey?"

"Yes sir, I mean, yes your Lordship. Thank you. I'll be off now". He made a small bow and trotted along the steep, narrow lane towards the church.

On previous occasions, he had knelt at the five barred gate into Griffe wood and defended himself against other hordes.

Not today.

The clock showed him to be ten minutes late already. But he couldn't help glancing into the field which ran alongside the lane. The devilish bands had melted away and the hayfield ocean ruffled magically under a slight breeze.

"Wait until father learns that I have been speaking to the Earl of Scarsdale! It isn't often that father meets him even though he rents the land out to us."

But for the time being, he had to face his tutors. The Reverend William Webster was standing in the shadow of the cemetery gate. A stern, upright figure in his black surplice, long nose pointed down the lane towards Peter.

Sutton Mill Farm

The rear of Peter Fidler's birthp;ace

Then Peter faltered in his stride. His homework! He had left it on the ground beside the horse!

And as he turned with heart of lead, he saw and heard the large horse galloping towards him.

Reginald Leake, the Earl of Scarsdale swept by, tossed the documents onto an area of clean grass, and sped past with a shout of "Halloo!" and a wave of an arm.

Peter recovered his documents and thrust them into his jerkin, then ran pell-mell towards the church gate.

Scarsdale's Proposal

A uniformed manservant opened the studded oaken door at Scarsdale Hall.

"Mr Fidler, ain't it?" he queried with an affected nasal voice.

Sutton Hill Farm
The front of Peter Fidler's birthplace

"Of course it is, Baz" replied James Fidler peevishly. "Why does thee always have to go through this palaver every time I comes here?"

Baz sniffed, made no immediate answer, but opened the door sufficient for James to enter.

"Come in then and scrape yer footwear

James did as he was bid. He removed his battered hat, scraped his boots on the scraper by the door and stepped inside. Everything shone and smelled of sweet oils although the great house was becoming dilapidated since the death of Nicholas Leake in 1724. His grandson, Reginald, Earl of Scarsdale, spent very little time at Scarsdale Hall.

"His Lordship's Steward is in the Long Hall. Follow me, he's expecting you"

Baz closed the door. Light streamed from vast stone-edged windows above them. The wooden floor gleamed. They walked along the narrow carpet towards another doorway.

The Long Hall of Scarsdale Hall stretched the length of a field. It had been used for a variety of purposes, including swordplay, tennis, bowls, wrestling, dinner parties, and more dubious activities in its time, but was quieter these days. A long, hand-made mahogany table, sturdy and functional, stretched along its centre.

In the middle, a high-backed, severe chair contained a man in dark suit. In the previous century, he could have passed as a high-ranking supporter of Oliver Cromwell, but today, in August 1782, he was a Royalist and Steward of the affairs of his master, the Earl of Scarsdale.

He looked up, smiled and waved to a seat alongside him.

"Come in, Mr Fidler, do come in. Be seated my dear fellow. And how are you today?"

James increased the speed of his stride slightly to reach the chair and sit stiffly alongside Captain Glasbye.

"Quite well thank thee Captain. Quite well. My wife sends her regards to thee and thine." Taking a parcel from beneath his arm he went on

"And here's the carrot cake that thy good lady likes"

"Why thank you as usual, James. I always like a piece of your wife's home-made cake. Return my regards to Mary "

He smacked his lips appreciatively.

"Right. Let's get down to business."

He balanced a pair of half-spectacles on his broad nose and flicked an imaginary dust mote from his frilled cuffs.

"I think we agreed two pounds seventeen and sixpence for this payment, did we not?"

He looked at James over the spectacles.

"We did, Captain, but I'm just a little short at this time. I can raise it later at the corn mill, as usual, but I've spent a bit of cash on my eldest lad's education. There's no problem, but I would just like a little more time. Peter'll be working with me soon, full hours, after his birthday on the 16th August and I reckon we can improve financial matters greatly".

He felt into a deep coat pocket

"There's two pounds twelve and sixpence and I'll pay the difference for the rent in three months. Is that alright?"

Glasbye continued to stare down at the heavy ledger. He moved his right hand forward and twiddled a large goose quill slotted against an inkwell.

Without commenting, he slid a hand inside his black astrakhan waistcoat pocket, removed a small jewelled case, and from it, helped himself to a pinch of snuff.

27

Tucked into a coat sleeve was a large, plain handkerchief, snuff stained, into which he sneezed several times.

"How old is Peter on his next birthday?" he enquired.

"Peter? Why he'll be, let me see. Er, 1769, that's thirteen. Yes, he'll be thirteen. Why does tha ask that?"

Glasbye turned, lifting the heavy chair so that he was facing James.

"I don't think it comes as any surprise to you to be told that his Lordship has taken a shine to Peter over the past few years, isn't that right?"

"Yes. That's right. I can't deny that. But what's that got to do with my rent?"

"Well. His Lordship is quite agreeably impressed by Peter. Thinks he's a very bright lad. Has potential. He instructed me to tell you that he is prepared to recommend him for a position with the Hudson's Bay Company. Not much to start with, of course, but if he works well he'll have all kinds of opportunities in the New World. His Lordship has spoken with Peter's tutor who is impressed by the boy's grasp of mathematics, including geometry and astronomy. He writes with a fine, legible hand. In other words, he could be as useful to the Company as to you. "

He continued to stare thoughtfully at the great ledger.

"You may be aware that his Lordship's son will be attending Saint Paul's School in London soon. He has suggested that Peter travel with him as body servant. "

He looked up.

"It means that Peter will be able to attend classes and finish his education, James. An opportunity that few youngsters get, don't you agree?".

James was stunned. His jaw hung down, mouth open.

"Well, you've got all year to think about it. He'll have to be at least fourteen before they'll take him, anyway. In the meantime, I have authority to agree with your proposals about deferring the rental for three months and I'll see you then. Alright? I'm happy about the village taxes, which I understood you collected and took to Chesterfield."

He pulled a sheet from inside the pages of the ledger.

"That's your mark, isn't it?"

James nodded numbly.

"While you are here, I ought to touch on the roadworks that are still outstanding. Is everything a well with the villagers? "

Every male villager was required to give three days unpaid work on road maintenance under the supervision of a village Constable.

James and later, his son James, were both Constables.

He had inherited the role from his wife's father Peter Glossop. James eldest son, Peter, was named after his maternal grandfather.

"The next bit of work includes some clearing on the footpath from the main road to the Hall" he said."I don't 'spect any problems"

Leaning over, he accepted the proffered ink-dipped quill and made his mark at the bottom of the ledger.

"Thank thee Captain. I'll do as tha says and think about matters. Good day to thee"

Standing up, he touched his forelock and walked as though in a dream towards the massive back door.

Baz smiled knowingly and closed the door behind him.

Turnor's Choice

Philip Turnor leaned against a door post of the trading fort at Cumberland House, well inland from York. He sipped a hot beverage whose fragrance suffused the inside of the cabin.

"What did you say this is, Charles?"

Charles Isham lounged in roughly hewn wooden chair with one leg dangling over the corner of a plank table.

"It's an Indian drink. They take it like tea. Can't remember the proper name, if I ever knew it! We just call it Indian Tea."

He sipped at his own drink.

"Very refreshing. If you use it, Philip, don't add anything. It's bloody poison! Ruins good rum or whisky and curdles milk. Got this batch a couple of weeks ago in the Swan River country, not far from Cedar Lake. The women pick it as leaves from some bush. Anyway, you don't want to hear these domestic trifles, I'm sure. I suppose I'll have to ask you why you've made this long trip. Was it just to see me?".

Turnor faced him.

"That's right Charles. I've had a communique from the Committee who want to implement our ideas. It's a chess game, really. "

He moved across the room to sit opposite Isham.

He untied then unrolled a parchment on the table, holding each corner using two mugs and two hunting knives.

"Here we are at Cumberland House". He pointed at the parchment map.

"But so are the North Westers. They come here then go across the Churchill River, up to Ile-a-la-Crosse, through Peter Pond Lake, and eventually descend the river to Lake Athabaska. It's a long, circuitous route but when they've arrived, they are straddled right across here, cutting our supply routes from the Indians to the West.

It's the route that their predecessor, Peter Pond was shown by the Indians and it's still used. "

He pointed to the middle of the area.

"You'll see that there's little marked there, Charles. But I believe it's possible to halve the travelling, probably by as much as 450 miles, by going across the centre. That would give us an edge on the Poachers at the early part of the season. I intend to survey that route from here to there, taking one of my new Assistants with me"

"I see. What do you want me to do?"

"I want you to go back to Swan River country and set up a canoe building industry to supply me and the rest of the Company with birch-bark canoes. There isn't such material available, as you know, along the route from York. I need them to go from York to Lake Athabaska in opposition to the NorthWesters. So you can bring them to me using the long route. Does that sound reasonable.. Charles?"

Isham moved a leg from the table and leaned forward to rub its calf.

"Sounds alright to me, Philip. When does this all start?"

"As soon as you think it's suitable for you to go, Charles.

Alexander Mackenzie is intent on driving a wedge between us and the Chipewyan Indians and any others that he can isolate us from. It's good business for both sides. Except us! We need posts right up against the Indians, and this will do it.

I'd like Mr Hudson to help me as Assistant, with young David Thompson as apprentice. He's gutsy and bright. Taken to Surveying like the proverbial fish to water. He's currently getting over a leg injury, but I'm hoping that he'll pick up during the next few months. You will remain in overall charge as the trader, but young Fidler can do the Writing here at Cumberland. Does that suit you?".

"Suits me fine, Philip. I have to say that this year is a write off, though. Mind you, I can make good use of those two lads as long as they are here"

Turnor nodded.

"The bark won't be ready until next Spring " he said

"So we have from now until then to prepare."

Turnor stood and stretched.

Isham stood as well, walked to the far wall and reached forwards. A section of the wall about two feet square, swung outwards. He reached inside and removed a stone jar..

"Join me in a night cap before we retire" he asked.

Turnor nodded, turned up the two mugs on the table and sat.

Chosen for the Wilderness

David Thompson turned up the wick on the oil lamp.

His face was thin and he looked unhappy.

Peter Fidler sat opposite him in their cosy cabin. Occasionally, a stiff breeze blew across the chimney stack, the fire fluttered and wood smoke puffed into the room. A small window with wooden shutter propped open was the means of egress for the woodsmoke.

David grimaced and kneaded his right thigh.

"Is it hurting, David?"

"Like a constant toothache that flares up every so often. I curse that steep bank every time I think of it and that's quite a lot!"

He rubbed the leg again.

"I curse me more, though. Stupid thing to do! And I hadn't been very long at Manchester House. Worst of all, it was Mr Tomison himself who arranged for me to be hauled home!"

He looked directly at Peter.

"I've an awful feeling that it won't be strong enough for the Lake Athabasca survey, Peter. Now Mr Turnor has started teaching you, I think that you will be the natural choice to take my place. I must confess that I hate the idea, but there's very little that I can do, is there?"

Peter said nothing, not wishing to cause further anguish to his friend.

"Well" said David after a while, "There are some things that I've been taught which you haven't, yet. If it's all right by you, I'll take you through them. Just in case. I'll teach you what I know about theory and then you can work out the latitude and longitude of Cumberland House. I've already done that, so I can check your results for you. I don't want to sound bossy, but I think it's a way of helping me, you and the Company. What do you think?"

"That would be very helpful, David", said Peter sadly.

31

Thompson leaned forward, painfully and pushed a book towards Peter. "Come on, me Bucko, cheer up! Try starting at page 25, Peter."

He was interrupted by loud laughter from outside and the crash of heavy boots on the wooden boardwalk.

A group of men, heavily armed, wearing leather jerkins and trousers trimmed with buffalo fur and racoon skin headgear stomped their boots as they walked towards the Company Store.

Peter peaked through the shutters and watched them enter.

They spoke in loud voices, predominantly Scots. One of them slammed the door of the store, hiding them from view.

"Who's that?" asked David.

"Nobody that I know," said Peter, "but I think that I can take a guess. I heard the Guv'nor mention last week that it was about time we had a visit from the NorthWest Company. They come through here every year, apparently on their way to rendezvous at Grand Portage. I don't know which is which, but he did mention Angus Shaw who built the first fur-trade post on Moose Lake. Then there was"

He stopped and thought for a moment.

"I think he said Patrick Small from Ile-a-la-Crosse, another called McGillivray and the one that's causing us trouble in the North West, Alex or Albert or something MacKenzie."

"Peter! Peter Fidler!"

A loud voice called from the Store.

"That's Mr Turnor. You'd better move, my bucko" said David.

Peter flung open the door and ran along the veranda to the large cabin to the side.

He rushed inside to be met by a group of steely facial expressions.

"Yessir" he gulped.

A bar with brass foot rail ran a quarter length of the cabin. Along the wall were jars and bottles containing a variety of drinks, especially whiskey and rum. Turnor was behind the crowded bar and four men leaned in different poses along it. Three had a foot on the rail. The fourth, a tall, black bearded, heavily set man whose red tartan shirt could be seen underneath his leathers, leaned back with elbows on the bar and with crossed feet. A thick, black beard fell to his chest.

"This is my latest trainee Assistant, gentlemen. Master Peter Fidler. Mr David Thompson is my other helper but he's indisposed at the moment".

He walked to the open end of the bar.

"Peter, meet the Masters of the Canadian Settlements to the North West.."

None smiled. None changed expression. One at the left lifted his glass and sipped it.

Peter gave a half bow. "Welcome to Cumberland House, gentlemen"

The heavily built one spoke. His voice was deep, with an educated Scots accent.

"So you're the next Hudson's Bay weapon that we should be wary of, are ye lad? And if you're anything as good as your master, then you'll do well"

He turned to the bar, picked up a tumbler filled with amber liquid and held it in front of his face, smoothing down his long beard with his free hand.

"Here's to ye Peter laddie and I hope your English sporran fills with gold"

The others laughed, including Turnor, who filled up empty glasses.

"These other gentlemen Peter, are Misters Small, Shaw and McGillivray. Note them well and always remember that however we compete, we are always white gentlemen who look after one another in Indian territory."

The visitors nodded in agreement.

Peter listened at the edge of the conversation.

"I hear you've tried to reach the Western Ocean, McKenzie" said Turnor.

"Aye. That I have, Turnor, but I think we met the edge of the Hypoborean Sea, not the real one. Mind you, we've wintered well both in respect of trade and provisions, so I'm happy at the outcome."

He addressed Peter.

"I'm told that you've learned some of the magic of surveying, Master Fidler. I can share with you that I'm learning it myself. When I come back from Scotland, I may ask you to join us, What would you say to that?

Turnor watched him.

"Not in a million years, sir. I owe what I have to my Company, but thank you for your graceful offer"

Turnor smiled and turned away with a nod to himself.

"Well, Turnor" said McGillivray, holding out a gloved hand, "Thanks for your hospitality. I hope we can respond in the normal way. We have been here since 2 o'clock and I think we are all eager to move on. It's four p.m, now, with enough summer light remaining for the next leg of the journey so, fare well. And you too, young Fidler. We may meet on the trail".

The men shook hands with Turnor and patted Peter on the head, arm or shoulder.

He muttered "Goodbye" as they passed through the doorway into afternoon light.

Turnor walked with them to the main gate of the post where a number of horses could be seen, together with some strange Indians that had not entered.

Small who had said little, bawled something in an Indian tongue and a bustling began among the outsiders.

Peter watched for as long as he dared then ran back to his cabin, jumping a horse rail and leap-frogging a hitching post to reach the broadwalk.

He burst in upon the startled David.

"Wait till I tell you about this afternoon" he said excitedly, "but first I want to make an entry in my diary before I forget.

He thumbed his way through to its next empty sheet and entered 'Wednesday June 20th 1790', talking all the while as he wrote.

"McKenzie said that he's started to learn surveying " he said to David as he finished the entry and closed his log.

"But I don't think that he understands enough about it at all from what he was saying. He didn't rightly know where he'd been, whether it was the Hyperborean Sea or the Western Ocean."

A boot scraped, the door opened and Turnor entered.

He looked from one to the other and back again.

"I've decided to make my way to Lake Athabasca and begin surveying. It hasn't been an easy decision, David, but under the circumstances, I can't wait and you can't get better any more quickly. So, it is with regret that I must tell you that on this occasion, you must stay here and look after the House until we return."

He turned to Peter.

"Peter, when I say we, I include you. You know enough to start, you can keep records and whatever else you need I can teach you on the way. "

He leaned against the wall.

"I expect to be ready by September, round about the second week. I shall head for Athapascow. I'll give you more detail as I finalise plans. Any questions?"

David looked close to tears.

Peter avoided looking at him and said

"Who else is going Mr Turnor?"

"Well, I haven't thought it right through yet, Peter, but I guess it will probably be Malcolm Ross as canoe master, Hugh Leask as steersman, Robert Garrock and Malcolm Grott. Not to mention me and you, of course. Oh! And I think I might invite Mr Ross and his woman. Perhaps one of the other women too, to keep her company. It's always useful to have an Indian woman along, to make shoes, cut lines, make netting snowshoes, cleaning and stretching skins, etcetera. All the necessary chores that Europeans are not acquainted with."

There being no more questions, he turned and opened the door, then hesitated.

"I know that you are friends as well as colleagues so be aware that this journey will keep us away for a year or so".

He smiled and strode into the weak afternoon sunshine.

Before Peter and David could open their mouths, Turnor was back in the doorway.

"I imagine that the question why we are going to the Athabascow will be asked by one of you. I think we need to survey that area to settle some dubious points.

I think that the Westers, Pond and Hearne fixed those place in their respective maps far more West than they really are. I'd like us to check it. That may be you job, Peter."

With which final remark, he swung around and was gone.

35

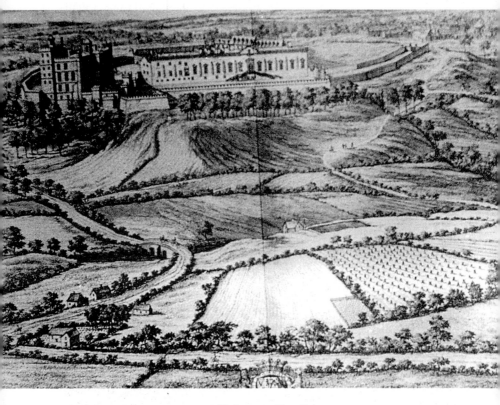

Bolsover Castle

An engraving made in 1695. The small house near the centre, at the side of Doe Lea Stream is Sutton Farm Mill.

CHAPTER 2

FiRsT JouRneys & AdventuRes

"I've been looking forward to this trip, David" said Peter.

"You know there'll be dangers and hardships, uncertainties ahead, but you'll cope with them" said David wistfully. "Be good, bucko and don't run off with any Indian maidens."

Peter clasped David's upper arm. "Well, not unless she's got a sister for you."

David smiled. " Anyway, she wouldn't have to run very fast to catch me!" and he nodded with a grimace at his long walking stick. "Which way will you be going?"

Philip Turnor surveying East Athabasca Lake in 1791 for the Honourable Hudson's Bay Company. Peter Fidler, on the left of the picture, is his Assistant Surveyor.

Original painting by Lorne Bouchard for the Hudson's Bay Company.

"Mr Turnor has decided that a guide will take us through Namew Lake, then Pelican Lake till we strike the Churchill River . None of us has taken this route before, least of all me!! So we nearly all know as much as each other!"

"Well, good luck, Peter. I can't say in all honesty that I'm glad that you're going instead of me, but it's no good crying over whatsit. Go and be careful. See you next year. Then it'll be my turn!"

Two canoes had been packed and the explorers, two women, several children and some dogs, were ready to go.

Peter saluted with a wave of his hand and ran across the compound, out of the gate and down to the water's edge.

The canoe master called for attention and everyone in the boats, including women and children began to paddle in unison, upstream towards the wilderness and the unknown.

"You'll find that paddling is hard work, especially against the fast running currents, some of which come from unexpected directions." Malcolm Ross told Peter," but you'll get used to it in time. When your arms begin to ache lad, or especially when you get a cramp in your side, switch places and go the other side"

At the end of the first day, Turnor had his canoe pulled into the side so that he could take bearings and he encouraged Peter to do the same.

"We'll camp a few miles down there tonight" said Ross, pointing ahead, "then you can take a wash and get some sleep. You'll keep the first watch"

"What watch?" asked Peter in between strokes.

Ross chuckled.

"Work doesn't finish when we pulls in to the shore" he explained. "No. We has to take the boats away from the water, make a fire, get something to eat, fresh if possible, but if not, it's the pemmican. Then we gets some shuteye. But everybody can't sleep. Oh no! That's too dangerous. So we takes turns overnight to keep a couple of hours watch for self-protection. See what I mean?"

Peter nodded and applied himself to the paddling. He decided to take bearings in the morning after he'd managed to grab a couple of hours sleep.

During his night watch, mosquitoes smelled him out and bit him mercilessly. He heard Indians creeping in the darkness behind every tree and bush and on one occasion he remembered running as a child through his hometown meadows, pursued by invisible savages. Perhaps it had been a portent of today's life?

Occasionally, he heard a twig crack as though by the weight of a body, but each one turned out to be a green branch on the fire.

The others were fanned out, wrapped in robes, in a circle around the warmth. His two hour watch seemed to last for ever and he jumped when Mr Leask, stood up.

"Take thy turn in bed now, Master Fidler" he whispered.

"Goodnight, Mr Leask" Peter mumbled and dropped into his buffalo sleeping bag, asleep before he knew it.

Dawn broke with a cacophony of sounds throughout the woodlands. The Indian women was toasting or roasting pemmican over a cheerful fire and one of the children passed a piece to him on a bark plate. He was ravenous and decided that he would have eaten it cold or hot.

"Right. " said Turnor. "We'll be continuing today as we did yesterday. I'm fairly happy with some of the observations that I've taken so far. Starting today, Peter, I want you to join me when we tie up and we'll make observations together. All right?"

Peter nodded.

"We are heading for Pelican Lake as we all know. The guide is in my canoe and Mr Ross is our interpreter. I want to strike the Churchill River some few miles east of Lac la Rouge then turn upstream. We shall be heading for Il-a-la-Crosse, to which I don't believe any of us has yet been. Certainly not by this route, anyway."

He looked around. Searching everyone's face, he nodded with satisfaction.

"We'll finish what we are doing and load up in fifteen minutes"

The day was a repetition of yesterday, and the day after was another repetition. Muscles ached, legs cramped, eyes misted. There were fewer mosquitoes out in the centre of the river, but the current was much stronger there.

Peter had taken a dozen readings and entered them in his journal.

Turnor was satisfied with the results and gave him more complex problems to solve. Peter wanted to look around and observe events, but his mind would insist on returning to the survey questions. Each night found him exhausted and he slept dreamlessly until they reached Pelican Lake on the fourth day.

Guide Goes and they Meet a Master.

"Goddamit to Hell!" bawled a loud voice.

Peter jumped up in alarm to find Ross standing straggle-legged at the spot where the guide had been.

"He's buggered off! During the night! I never did trust the sod!"

"What's happened?" demanded Turnor pushing through the willow bushes.

"It's that bloody guide, Mr Turnor. He's slung his hook!"

Turnor stood still, his face deep in thought. No emotions or anxiety showed.

"Right" he said."We need to cross the lake, I know, so we'll go across, make camp and think out our next move for tomorrow. But let's have a good look round for the rogue in the meantime. I'll meet everyone at this spot in an hour. All right?"

An hour later, all had returned without any sign of the guide.

"He's definitely deserted" said Mr Leask. "Problem is, you don't know why they does it!"

The canoes were loaded, and Turnor took the lead canoe.

"Stay in touch" he said and made a cavalry movement with his arm.

Pelican Lake was wider than it looked.

What must have been half way across, Turnor shouted and waved an arm. The paddlers stopped.

"Over there!" he called, pointing.

Three canoes were approaching them from the East.

Men looked to their weapons and made sure they were handy,

Turnor shouted again. It sounded like

"It's very small!"

"What's very small?" asked the puzzled Peter.

"Dunno" said Leask.

Turnor, seeing that the people in the other canoe had not understood, shouted louder.

"It's, Mister Small! The North Westers!"

The two groups drew together until they were almost within touching distance.

"Good day to ye Turnor. What are ye doing out here, so far?"

"Good day Mister Small. And a lovely one it is, too. We are planning on visiting Isle-a-la-Crosse. Would you like to accompany us? We would

40

be pleasured to travel with you if you are going our way".

Patrick Small, with a physique anything but small, scowled ferociously.

"To Isle-a-la-Crosse ? True that's where we are headed but I see no guide in your boats who can take you".

He nodded contemptuously towards the Indian women.

"They'll be no good. Their tribe's not from the area. So how did you intend to do it alone? It will take even us another month before we arrive and all my men know the route".

"Indeed, sir. But don't forget that we are Surveyors, trained to find our way in the wilderness. And, may I remind you, that I was the first to survey the Churchill River?" He stopped speaking briefly, then said

"But if it disaccommodates you, Mr Small, then we would not wish to impose ourselves upon you. Indeed not! So we will bid you well met, sir, and continue our journey. We expect to see you there"

He hesitated briefly

"During the first week in October"

He turned and leaned forwards to retrieve his paddle.

Small frowned even more.

"Wait a minute, Turnor. I did'na say that we did' na want your company, man. Och. Well. I suppose we'd better go together. Come along if you will. My boat will take the lead. But I must have your word that you will do no trade for skins with any Indians along the route!"

"Done!" said Turnor instantly "But I do hope you'll forgive me and young Fidler there, for confirming our records as we proceed?"

Small grunted. A hard business man, a shrewd manager a brave, unscrupulous entrepeneur, such records meant nothing to him.

It soon became apparent that without a guide, Turnor's party could have become hopelessly confused by the innumerable conflicting channels and inlets. Winter was fast approaching and their party had insufficient provisions to last them through the winter in a hostile environment.

The trading fort of Isle-a-la-Crosse was sighted at dawn on the 7th October meeting the wild and arbitrary arrival date calculated by Turnor.

There were Indians everywhere. Peter realised there were tribal differences, but he was yet to learn them.

Mr Small spoke to two swarthy white men at the landing and beckoned to Turnor.

"Take your men with Ryan " he called, pointing at one of the men who wore a drooping, wide-brimmed leather hat.

"Ye can put your men in one of the Company houses that he'll show you. " With which parting instruction, he walked away and entered a log building.

Ryan looked strong and wiry. He made no effort to help them and waited patiently until everything was removed from the canoes and they were lifted above a flood line.

He jerked his head and strode off lithely towards another group of cabins. In front of the first building he stopped and pointed to its door.

"It's up to you whether you take the squaws and their brats or not" he said suddenly. "They normally stay outside"

Without waiting for an answer, he spun on his heel, spat contemptuously and ambled back to the canoes.

"Perhaps you'll be kind enough to help the children, Mr Ross?" said Turnor quietly, placing a restraining hand on him.

Ross had turned red with rage at Ryan's remark and would have gone after him had Turnor not intervened.

Ross swallowed hard, picked up a satchel and shepherded the children inside.

Later that day, the men gathered around a pot-bellied stove whose cast iron chimney passed through the wall.

It was a luxurious item so far from European civilisation. Its top was cherry red and heat radiated out in all directions, but particularly through its open door.

A tortoise was cast into the circular lid and beneath it was proclaimed 'slow but sure'.

Turnor was speaking in an undertone.

"Perhaps some of you were unaware that provisions have been very tight, thus far.

With the exception of Peter and myself, you were supplied with Scotch Barley, oatmeal, Flour and Salt. We two had some Flour but none of the other articles."

He looked around at the silent group.

"We can't say that we have the promise of over-abundance of vittels even with what our hosts will provide for us. It's likely to be a lean winter. The normal fare here will be fish. Some of the younger men will have to hunt for the group and themselves to ease the strain on our larder."

"Who do you expect that will be, Mr Turnor?" asked Hugh Leask.

"I think I can trust you to do that, Hugh assisted by Peter, I reckon. You will have noticed that there is a number of Chippewyans here. I'd like Peter at least to pick up a working knowledge of their language. You too, if you want."

Hugh Leask shook his head and smiled.

"Not my cuppa tea, sir" he said. "Leaves that sort of thing to these young educated lads. Can manage to learn the names of things, but there's plenty other things I can do"

Turnor smiled and nodded.

"I want you to work out towards Knee Lake and Primrose Lake, north of here. It will be very important to establish cordial relations with the Chippewyans"

Peter's imagination took him back for fleeting moments to his home of three years before. The cosy civilisation of coal-rich Bolsover, England, could hardly have been more different than the cold climate of northern Saskatchewan, hunger, Indians, with the chance of visiting one of their camps.

"When do you suggest that we go, sir" asked Peter.

"I'll finalise that with Mr Leask, but I think sometime about twelve weeks hence. That makes it somewhere in the middle of January, I estimate"

Hugh Leask was counting on his fingers.

"Be about the second or third week, I guess and unless we need to do something earlier, we should be back before the end of April "

"Right. Well, let's get ourselves sorted into working units. I still want you to practice your magic, Peter" and he smiled.

Peter began working with a will. No amount of hunger was going to dampen his enthusiasm for the unknown and its excitement.

Return to Base

It was the middle of April of a new year, 1791. Winter had passed. Snow was melting rapidly. Rivulets ran through still frozen streams, wearing grooves and holes in the icy surfaces. Fidler, Leask and their Chippewyans returned to the post, the former looking leaner but fitter than when they left in January.

Welcome back, lads, welcome back! " cried Turnor, meeting them beyond the gate and shaking their hands several times. The Indians grinned gleefully and shook hands with one another.

You look fine, but a good steak should help you!"

The men, Indians and all, still swathed in furs, sat outside in the weak sunshine, greedily devouring slices of tender moose meat. Dogs snarled, rushed and snapped at one another between their heavily moccassined feet or yelped at a thoughtless kick. The smell of barbecued meat filled the compound and squaws dished out piled platters of it.

That'll square you up" said Turnor gleefully."Fatten you up for our next venture".

Leask and Fidler stopped eating and looked at him.

"Next venture? Already? We've only just walked in " said Leask.

"Not immediately, lads. No, not immediately. But we've been straining at the leash here while you've been out there enjoying yourselves. No, not immediately, but in about a month. Say the end of May"

The month passed quickly. Peter readjusted himself to the Isle-a-la-Crosse routine

"It's not that they've said anything about it" remarked Turnor, "but it's now the final week in May and I think they want rid of us. I must say they have done well by us and I shan't forget it. But I can feel a nervous energy from them that wishes goodbye"

He was leaning at their cabin doorway, watching Indians stacking sleds and organising dogs.

He sipped at his Indian tea.

Peter, Ross and Leask leaned on a hitching rail, chest high around the front of the building.

Ross used a horn handled knife with very heavy blade to whittle points to long lengths of sapling.

"It's the 30th of May on Monday next, and I want to be leaving then, provided the lake is open. All the signs indicate that it will be, but we can't discount one of those sudden, seasonal snaps of frost. If that happens, we'll decide on another date"

"I need a new compass" said Peter, his head held low "

"A new compass! What's wrong with your old one? And where do you expect to find a replacement out here?. This is not London you know!"

Turnor showed one of his rare moments of anger.

"Sorry, Philip" mumbled Peter

44

"Being sorry is not enough, young fella- me-lad! I trust that you will take this as an object lesson. Such so called 'accidents' are caused by lack of care, Peter, and one of the first requirements of a surveyor in this country is to be long on foresight and short on accidents"

He flung the remains of the tea onto the unmade road and stomped inside the cabin.

Peter remained silent, a hurt expression on his face.

"Well, I must say that you've had a good telling off, lad" said Ross. "But the guv'nor is right, you know." He paused.

"Will it still work?" he asked.

"It will do if I get a new glass" said Peter.

"Well then, put a bright face on things. A week tomorrow we should be somewhere near the south end of Lake Churchill, I estimate. But then not being one of the magical few my guess is not as good as yours! I 'spects as how we'll be hopelessly lost because you bust your compass!" He and Leask laughed uproariously and slapped Peter on the back, who grinned sheepishly, red-faced.

When they were near the south end of Churchill Lake, they stopped at an abandoned cabin.

"This must have been built last autumn by the Canadians to keep the Indians from creeping up on Isle-a-la-Crosse" said Ross watching his squaw poking and examining likely prizes.

"Who exactly are the Canadians" asked Peter "I've heard it used often enough, of course, but I couldn't give anybody a definite description."

"It means almost anybody from the North West Company, but only white men. Indians is whatever they is, Chipewyans, Cree, Plains and lots of others. It also means the independents that comes mainly from, Mount Royal. They calls that Montreal, now though. Them that Mr Tomison gets angered at and calls 'poachers'. Yep. They's all Canadians.

Problem is, lad, there's an awful lot of 'em.They numbers more than us. It means as they can be sent out in all directions to poach our trade before the Indians can reach our posts"

"We'll camp here tonight, lads" said Turnor, pushing some notes into a deep side pocket. "We'll be leaving at sun up as usual, so get your rest."

"It's the glorious first of June tomorrow" said Leask.

"Why do they call it the glorious first, Hugh?"

"Dunno" said Leask tartly. "How should I know?" and he bustled away, grumbling to himself.

Five a.m. found them into Peter Pond Lake. They continued all day until 6.30 p.m., a long day and a long pull.

Camp fires burned well, when there was a shout from around the river bend. The men jumped up and took defensive positions.

Around the headland swung a canoe with a white man in bright red tartan shirt and long black beard. McKenzie, sweeping down from the north.

He leaped from the canoe as soon as the forefoot touched sand.

"Well, well, well Turnor. So you are here! I thought it was you, but I wasn't sure"

He looked around.

"The fires look inviting and something smells good"

Turnor said "Glad to see you McKenzie. Make what arrangements you like with your men and accept our hospitality. Eat what you will and sit where you will".

McKenzie barked instructions to his Indians. They chattered and drew the canoe from the lake, then made themselves comfortable some yards away from the Europeans.

"Notice that a couple of 'em have gone into the woods, lad" whispered Leask. "Allus do that, they do. Covers their mates' backs from anybody creeping about inland"

Turnor and McKenzie were chewing at large lumps of cooked meat.

"I've had a glance around your camp, laddie and I'm a wee bit worried at what I see"

"And what do you see, McKenzie?"

"Weel, you're not over provisioned are ye? And there's very little game along this route. It been cleared of game over the years."

McKenzie stopped, then said thoughtfully

"Unless you know something I don't and you've got another route in mind?"

"Let's look at it this way, McKenzie. You look as though you're on an exploratory expedition. Now, several of us are already Surveyors. We know exactly where we are, where we've been and where we are going. I suggest that your inability to record where you are etcetera is a distinct defect in your project. I remember the last time we met, you were learning surveying. how far have you got with it?"

"Aye. So I was. But I've not had the time. However, I take your point, and I shall be going to England this year for that very reason, when this bit of business is finished." He smiled grimly. "I expect to learn enough about the art to meet you on your own ground, Turnor!".

McKenzie threw a half gnawed bone into the undergrowth where it was pursued by a pair of dogs

"I can only make this a short visit, my friend, so I shall be away early in the morning. Before dawn."

He stood, brushed himself down, smoothed his beard which showed signs of dripped fat, belched loudly and joined his Indians.

Turnor joined his own crew.

"Any news of importance, guv'nor?" asked Mr Leask.

Turnor nodded.

"They'll be leaving early tomorrow morning, probably about three o'clock. I doubt if we'll manage that hour. Our Chippewyans don't like getting up in the morning, which is why we are normally later than I'd prefer."

He sat on a log and gazed into the fire.

"We'll ascend the Methy River. McKenzie said that buffalo tracks had been reported there but, even so, I don't want to go near Methy Portage. There's a route I've heard of which no Europeans have used before, I believe, which goes up Garson River to a lake, Garson Lake I believe."

Peter listened whilst grinding a piece of glass against a hard stone from the river bank .

"What you doin', lad? " asked Mr Leask.

"I'm making a new glass for my compass" said Peter.

"Well done!" commented Turnor.

"So, I'll wise you up as usual about my intentions"

He took one of Ross's long, pointed sticks and made marks on the open ground.

"We shall have to do a bit of portage from Garson Lake to Formby Lake, which drains into the Athabasca River. I'm not sure what's in between, but we'll find out soon enough. I'm expecting that we can get to the Christina by this route".

He laid down the stick neatly, alongside his feet and pointing to the fire.

"Anybody have any questions"

There were none.

Portage: ascending the Athabasca River.

Artist: FAH (Provincial Arhives)

Indians, Tar, Coal & Fossils

They carried canoes and equipment overland as Turnor had reckoned. They were pleased to embark and follow the waters from Formby Lake and the Newby River and past Winefred River into the Christina.

"Mr Turnor and his Indians have gone ashore" observed Peter.

His face was peeling with sunburn and he had rubbed fat into his face, neck and hands to protect them from sun and mosquitoes.

"I think they've seen some deer tracks, or something like that" said Mr Leask, huddled over the side of the canoe, rinsing his mouth in the sparkling water.

A shout of triumph echoed through the trees and within minutes, the landing party came down to their canoe. The body of a moose was dragged in a human travois by two Indians who staggered under its weight. Before Peter's crew had reached the shore and beached their canoe, the others had begun a fire, skinned the moose and were drying it.

Large pieces that were left over made the current meal.

"Wonder what's a matter with they, then!" Leask queried, pointing a bone in the direction of Ross.

The acknowledged senior of the Indians had wrapped a blanket around himself and was talking to Ross. His movements were animated and jerky so that it looked sometimes as though he was trying to fly, using the blanket as wings.

Ross nodded and made the sign for 'Thank you. End of conversation' then walked over to Turnor, who had been watching, and squatted down beside him.

"Something's up!" said Leask.

Eventually, Turnor stood up and walked towards his crew gathered around the fire.

"You probably all noticed Ross talking with the Indian guide. The Indians are not happy about going to the Christina, now they know where we are venturing. In their opinion, it's too dangerous. Rough water. Terrible and impassable rapids. Ross can't determine whether they are merely fed-up with the journey or really are worried and genuinely concerned about our safety!"

"What do you intend, Guv'nor" said Leask.

"We shall be going on, Hugh. If they decided not to accompany us, then we'll take one canoe and portage where we have to. Any questions?".

Peter had a million but none that he cared to ask.

Ross had returned to the small, glum Indian group.

He turned away from them, caught Turnor's eye and gave a thumbs up sign. Turnor gave a sigh of relief.

"It looks as though Mr Ross has persuaded them" he said, smiling."We'll soon see whether we have a major or a minor problem"

It was a minor problem. They were obliged to disembark and portage the boats on a few occasions, but very few.

"What's all that black strata" Peter asked Leask, pointing to the deeply scoured banks while they took a breather.

"Not sure" said Leask, "But remembers somebody mentioning it some while ago. Few years. 'Til the North Westers interrupted it, we did a lot more trade with the Crees, who bartered with the Beaver Indians. Sort of middlemen, I guess. One of the Crees, Wa-pa-su, 'The Swan', brought a sample of 'gum-that-flows-from-riverbank'. I think it was this stuff."

He rubbed a bruised shoulder.

"Peter Pond came this way many years ago. I think it might have been him who said about it. Never wrote it down though, so far as I know"

That night, Peter wrote in his journal

"Found great quantities of bitumen, a kind of liquid tar, pouring out of the banks on both sides of the river in many places, which has a very sulphurous smell and quite black like real tar and in my opinion would be a good substitute for that useful material"

Other interesting and unusual items caught Peter's attention.

He pointed at the steep river banks on another occasion.

"Look at those fossils" he said to Leask."Some of them seem to be in the middle of solid stone or are petrified to stone. What do you make them out to be, Hugh? They look like cockles and mussels and whelks and things."

"I suspect your right, lad" was Leask's contribution.

When they rested, Peter's youthful curiosity took him along the river bank to examine tar and fossils. At one point, he drank from a gushing spring, only to spit it out calling "Ugh! It's salt!".

Less than half an hour later, he had to call for a halt. The canoe was placed down carefully and Peter used some grease and soap to wash his black legs.

"How did you get like that, lad?" asked Leask incredulously, pointing at Peter's swollen feet and legs.

"I made the mistake of walking bare footed through a stream of pure, flowing bitumen, about ten inches deep, Hugh, at the last stop. It's itching and burning like mad!"

"I don't know what to suggest, young un, but be careful of 'em. There's a long way to go yet"

Peter nodded, splashed water onto his legs and took his weight of the canoe.

"That's a welcome sign" said Hugh, trying to take Peter's attention away from his aching legs and feet. "Buffalo tracks down to the water's edge. Fresh too.

And there's a house in the distance. Wonder who lives there?"

"It looks like the mouth of a river" panted Peter. "About 100 yards across. Wonder which one it is?"

"There's no smoke from the chimney" said Hugh more interested in the cabin than yet another river.

"Have you noticed the number of big birch trees along this bank?" said Peter suddenly. "Much bigger than the ones we get to the East."

"Yeah. Noticed" said Hugh "It only means they can make bigger and heavier canoes for us to carry!"

They floated the canoes and paddled across to the deserted cabin.

"It's about three years old, 1788" said Peter, reading some etchings in the porch.

"It's 21st June, 1791 today."

He paused and thought then said lamely

"I think so, anyway!"

"What's that bit say, just there Peter?" said Hugh pointing.

Peter peered closely. "I missed that, Hugh. It's the owner's name, I would guess. Looks like 'McLeod' "

Hugh stepped back and examined the building.

"It's a fair size, I reckon. Been used for trading, too."

He strode out the length and shouted over his shoulder "About thirty six feet by twenty. That roof holding the split logs is about seven feet off the ground, which means that centre ridgepole is about twelve feet. Decent sized place, all right"

"Looks as though somebody meant it to stay here for a while" said Peter. He peered into the darkness inside.

The place was empty, but the faint outlines of a table and benches could be seen.

"That's right, Peter. They've gone to great trouble to lay a split log floor and divided the place up into three by building walls."

"Why three rooms" asked Peter.

"Well, it's a fairly standard set up, lad. One part is for furs and provisions and the like, the middle bit here, is for trading with the Indians and the other part is called the guardroom. That's where the traders live."

Hugh moved closer to Peter, looked around then said in an undertone

"Don't say anything to Malcolm Ross unless he mentions it to your first, but I think this might be the place where his cousin, John Ross was killed."

He looked around furtively again.

"Though it might be another place not far from here. That date on the doorway is a bit confusin' as I believe it was the winter of '86 to '89 when it happened. It was murder, really, even though it was an accident"

"Murder?" said Peter, wide eyed "You mean that John Ross was murdered?"

"Been a few of those, Peter. Be some more I don't doubt. It's how the trade started. Hard men, unscrupulous men. Took what they wanted without so much as a by-you-leave"

He pulled a large, spotted kerchief from inside a deep pocket and wiped his face.

"You've heard of Peter Pond?"

Peter nodded.

"Well, Pond had already killed at least one man about six years before. He got his men to rob John of his furs. In open daylight, too! There was a Frenchie voyageur there named Peke, or Pesh or something like that. One of Pond's men, anyway. He was robbin' John and threatening him with a pistol, when it went off. Unexpected like! It killed poor John. I can't recall whether they took his furs or not, but they'd hardly be able to claim it as an accident if they did!"

"What happened to the Frenchie, then, Hugh?"

"Don't likely recall if he's still around or not " said Leask, scratching one side of his head. " An' he was the only Wester who could speak Jebewyan. He took off and lived with them for three summers and winters before he dare come back. Gallows was waitin' for him, you see. And Pond wasn't very popular in Montreal by all accounts. They didn't cotton on to traders who competed by killing the opposition! I think they sent Alex McKenzie to see him. Pond left the next year and McKenzie picked up where Pond left off."

Peter stopped, winced with pain and reached down to touch his feet.

"Are they still paining you, lad?"

"'Fraid so, Hugh. They don't seem to be getting better. I've got blisters all over my feet, now. I hate complaining, but I can hardly pick them up to get into the canoe. And as for walking, well, you can imagine!"

"What's the matter with your feet, Peter?"

Hugh and Peter jumped at the unexpected voice behind them.

Turnor had walked around the log house.

"He's just telling me about his burnt feet, Philip."

"I'll be alright" said Peter defensively, but unable to keep a spasm of pain from registering on his face.

"If you can hold out for three days, youngster" said Turnor "We'll be at Fort Chipewyan. Mr MacKenzie's relative, Mr Roderick MacKenzie is in charge and I have a letter for him. We should be able to alleviate your distress then. Can you manage to wait that long?"

"Of course, Mr Turnor. I don't want to hold us up" and he thought for a moment of David Thompson's predicament.

"If we've all eaten and are prepared, then let us embark" said Philip. "Hugh, will you give Peter a hand at embarking and, if necessary, disembarking, please?"

Three days travelled slowly for Peter. He wrote

"Feet so bad that I am obliged to be carried in and out of the canoe".

"You'll get a bit over rest over there" said Hugh, nodding towards a blockhouse that had come into view.

"It is a very cheering sight, Hugh" said Peter, thankfully and applied himself to paddling with new vigour.

After a few days, Peter's feet had healed enough for him to think of continuing with Turnor

"It's the end of June, Peter and Mr Turnor has returned from the mouth of Slave River where he's been taking the latitude and longitude." said Malcolm Ross.

"I've told him that you are well enough to crawl about now, and he says that's good and that you'll probably be more use like that than you've ever been!"

He laughed uproariously and slapped a thigh.

"So, you'll be goin' with him to East Athabasca Lake and I'll be building a new trading post for the Company near Fort Chipewyan"

He removed one glove and scratched his nose.

"Haven't decided what to call it yet, but it might be Athapascow House. My missus likes that name. It'll be the first Hudson Bay Company House on the Athabasca watershed. My men are arriving within the next few days, so it should be well on the way to finishin' by fall."

He put his glove back on.

"I says 'house' but it'll be two buildings. One for me and the missus with a part for warehousing and trading, with the other house partitioned in two A guardhouse for the men and an apartment for Mr Turnor".

Peter had remained silent through Malcolm's speech.

"Any idea when he's planning on going, Malcolm?"

"Think so. It should be this week, sometime, but he'll no doubt let us know in good time. He said that he wants to be back by the end of July"

They returned from surveying the East Athabasca Lake on 30th July.

"They are making a good job of the House" said Turnor as they approached. "We can get quite close inland the way they've contrived it"

The canoe was lifted on shore as usual and Turnor strode towards the partially completed buildings, meeting Ross half way.

Peter walked cautiously behind, favouring his healing feet.

"You'll be alright here for the winter, Peter" said Ross good humouredly, "Welcome to Athapascow House!"

"I wanted to talk to you about that" said Turnor .

Ross looked deflated.

"Don't you like the name then, Philip?"

"Oh! No, no, no! Sorry Malcolm. I didn't mean that. No. It's a lovely name. I meant about young Fidler being here for winter"

Peter had drawn next to them.

"I've been talking to Mr Turnor, Malcolm and I'd like to winter with the Chippewyans if that's all right. I need to learn their language more. I think I'll be fit enough and you know I can put up with almost any kind of living. I mean eating and drinking and such."

He looked from one to the other

"I don't drink, anyway" he said apologetically.

"The Indians are leaving in four canoes in a few days, probably the fourth of September. I can fix that you accompany them to Slave Lake"

"You realise that you'll be the only Hudson Bay man, Peter? And these Northern Indians live very close to the poverty line, as you know from previous contact. You'll have to live off the land as they do."

"Yes, Phillip, I understand and I still want to go"

"Very well." Turning to Ross. "Fix it then, please, Malcolm. I'll arrange for surveying materials, Nautical Tables and suchlike. I think you'll need a clean shirt, too!"

He faced Peter directly. "I'll tell you what I think, Mister Fidler. You are 21 years of age, loyal and courageous. I wish you well and will be happy to welcome you at the end of your adventure, next year"

He held out his hand and Peter shook it

CHAPTER 3

Among The Chipewyans Indians

(1791 - 1792)

The Chipewyan canoesmen were already in their boats when Ross and Fidler arrived.

Ross slung a large satchel in the stern of one canoe and Fidler placed one carefully in the other.

"Good luck, boy" said Ross, shaking Peter's hand.

"You can do a task for me while you are about it."

He nodded at the canoes, all of which had trade goods piled along the inside, covered with blankets.

"They've obtained a large credit in goods and I want you to keep an eye on them. Especially make sure they don't get parted from them by the Northwesters!"

He leaned forward and pulled aggravatedly at one of his boots.

"Which way are you going" he asked.

"I'm going down the Slave River and I want to take some readings. I think I shall have a bit of trouble without any parallel glasses, but I'll make do the best I can."

He looked over his shoulder at the impassive Indians.

"Thanks for everything, Malcolm and I'll see you next year"

He stepped into the nearest canoe, picked up a paddle and prepared to help. The steersman said something and a nearby crewman gently took it away from him.

"Don't look as though you're good enough to join their racing crew" said Ross with a laugh.

Peter waved and they were off.

He practised his Chipewyan language on the paddlers either side of him. It seemed as good a time as any to do so. Whenever the fancy took him which was often, he took bearings, made observations and transferred the information to his journal.

"The wind is rising" he said to his neighbour in front.

The Indian turned his head slightly, showing a scar on his left cheek, and grunted assent.

The lead canoe slowed, swung sideways and its steersmen shouted something.

"What shouts the steersman?" asked Peter.

"He shouts to warn us that there is a party of canoes ahead. Strangers"

"What is the name of that river?" asked Peter, pointing to a nearby inlet.

"That is the river of Peace" said his neighbour. He was polite, but more interested in the strange canoes.

"Peace River" said Peter aloud and wrote the name in his journal.

"Crees" said the man behind him, laconically.

The leader of Peter's group balanced himself upright in his canoe and made the greeting to strangers, customary to all tribes.

There was a jabber of excited conversation among
Peter's colleagues.

"Do you speak any of their foreign talk" the Chipewyan leader asked Peter?

"Not good. But plenty small talk. I talk to them. They may understand me".

The Crees had spotted Peter and were talking animatedly among themselves. White men were not common in Chipewyan canoes.

After traditional greeting, the Cree leader said

"Are you with these Northerners or are you a prisoner?"

"Not prisoner" replied Peter "Friend. I go live their winter lodge." He looked around for a subject of discussion which he could handle.

"Wind little big. Get more big, later"

"Yes. That's so" said the Cree, "We are hoping to avoid it on the way home. We go in the opposite direction to you"

"Opposite? Oh yes. Opposite. I understand"

He overheard a comment in the boat made by his Chipewyan steersman.

"They can't understand our language" the steersman said "These foreigners. We are more in number than they are. I agree that we should kill them all and share their goods."

"What will the signal be?" asked another.

"Wait a minute. Wait a minute!" said Peter, lapsing into a mixture of English and broken Chipewyan, trying not to look alarmed. "You can't just kill and rob them. I couldn't stand for that. If you do, then you'll have to kill me, because I shall be obliged to inform the authorities." He paused and entered the Chipewyan language again. His words were stilted, occasionally disconnected, but the message struck home. If they killed the Crees, they must kill Peter, for whom they had respect and they would be unlikely to trade with Hudson's Bay again.

The moment passed. Peter turned, suppressing a sigh of relief. The Crees had waited patiently without understanding a word by the Chipewyans.

After a while, and further small talk, the Crees waved goodbye and left, never realising how close to death they had been.

"There is no game along this river" said the neighbour. "We shall eat little for the next few days."

He was right. It was on the third day when they landed to hunt for anything edible that one of the foraging Indians came into the camp waving a partridge.

It was small for ten of them, but it was divided up.

"This for you" said the leader, holding a piece of bark on which was a whole partridge leg.

"All of that?" said Peter. It was a most generous portion.

"We go from here down Buffalo River to Great Slave Lake" said the leader. "We catch plenty beaver. Not fur this time. No. We eat plenty"

He gazed around, taking in weather signs.

"Maybe we shall stay closer to middle of river on this journey. Weather still cold. "

Peter puzzled about the enigmatic relationship between 'closer to middle of river' and the 'cold weather' until they reached the Lake.

It was frozen over for more than a mile from shore.

"What will happen now?" he asked his front neighbour.

"We shall wait until the ice is solid enough to walk on or melts. Probably the former" said the paddler. "Then we shall go to Moose Island. Beyond that is a North Westers' trading post" He looked pointedly at Peter's dilapidated condition.

" Perhaps they will trade you some white men's clothes"

Peter looked at himself.

"You are right, of course. This is the only shirt I have left and it's in a very poor condition" he said, poking at it.

"And I have no shoes or socks or mittens or anything to make them with. I have the small blanket you gave me and a moose skin. I may be able to trade them for something to wear"

When they arrived at the post, Peter's first thought was to acquire some clothing. The Northwester wasn't very interested but finally gave Peter some items.

"What did you get?" said the leader.

"Not a lot, but better than nothing." He held them out

"A pair of shoes, two old socks and about nine inches of worsted cloth"

"Hmm" said the leader. "I can't make a habit of it but I can lend you a blanket".

"That will be most gratefully received" said Peter, thankfully.

The Chipewyan were camping in large numbers around the post, but were obliged to pack up and move to hunt for food and fuel.

"We have plenty of fish" said the leader, "But we need some red meat before the middle of winter"

It was a few days later, in November, that a distant 'yipping' was heard. Braves and squaws rushed from their shelters to greet incoming hunters, several of whom trotted with a wooden travois on which was a large, buffalo cow.

"Plenty of broth today" said the leader who had moved silently alongside Peter.

Several women were digging a hole about two feet wide and one foot deep.

The braves had turned their backs on the kill and stalked jauntily away. Women descended on the carcase, chattering shrilly, and butchered it expertly. Each knew what the other was doing.

Two women cut out the animal's paunch and after cleaning it, suspended it on sticks set around the hole so that it hung down. The mouth was propped open with a cross of two, long sticks. The bones of the beast were broken up and marrow extracted. The fat was placed in the new fashioned kettle and other women placed hot stones inside it, which were changed frequently.

Eventually the mixture boiled then simmered, becoming a very nutritious broth.

All of them, including Peter, had hauled large stones during the week and he was introduced to yet another purpose for them. They had already been used for making fresh water from melting snow and ice.

The next day, talking to the Chief, he was told that winter would come quickly

"It will not be a friendly one, Peter. I know that you have borrowed my blanket, but that is not enough. One of my men has a whole deer skin to spare and he would like you to have it before it is wasted"

Peter was almost overwhelmed at the generosity and thoughtfulness of the unknown benefactor and thanked the Chief in the proper manner.

"I shall go straight away to my tent and make a coat" he said, fingering the softened material.

"Perhaps you can do something else with this, too" said the Chief, bending to pick up a rolled piece of the buffalo hide. "It is not much, but it may provide you with some leggings"

Peter could hardly contain himself. He used the buffalo to make a pair of trousers.

He was still poorly attired for a severe winter, but he continued mapping and making astronomical observations

"What has happened to your hands?" asked the Chief one morning in January.

" I was taking some star readings when my finger ends became severely frozen, I think" said Peter, pulling a face.

"Let me ask our Medicine Man to help you" said the Chief.

A little later, the Medicine Man smeared the fingers with a sweet-smelling paste.

"Leave that on" he instructed, "But more important, don't do it again!"

Peter felt told off, until his doctor said

"Your use of our language has become very good, Peter"

"Thank you" said Peter, with pleasure."I haven't mentioned it to any-one yet, but I think my dreams are in your language. I seem to have a larger range of words when I'm asleep than when I'm awake!"

"We shall be moving again in the morning" said the Chief "Over to the other side of Slave River. There are some more of our tribe over there that you haven't met yet. We are going because I've been told that they are in a poor way. Food is very scarce for them. We have not fared too badly, but we are better off than they are. If we can help, then we must do so".

Within hours of crossing, the Chief called the large party to a halt.

"You four, accompany me" he said to braves around him. "Peter. You come along with the Medicine Man"

They moved forward slowly towards a figure slumped at the base of a large rock. It was a woman, emaciated, starving, but very pregnant. Beside her, partially hidden by the rock, were the legs of a man. He was dead and had died cradling a boy, probably twelve year's old.

If Peter had been concerned about his own clothing, he became more concerned about the clothing of his colleagues. To show individual grief over the loss of the deceased they cut up their clothing, although they had none to spare. They howled and lamented all night. Peter reckoned in his journal that it was the worst night's sleep he had ever had!

The winter passed, hard and remorseless.

The starving woman went along with them.

"Isn't that the woman we found?" Peter said to one of the party.

"It is " he was told.

"But I understood that she had a child, recently" said Peter.

"She did" said the brave. "The women wanted to erect a small tent for her to have the child, but were too late. She had it yesterday, between the harness of her sleigh. A fine boy. Surprising really"

"But it's only yesterday since that happened!"

The brave looked surprised, then shrugged at the strange ideas of white men.

"Of course. She's had the child, thanks to the Great Spirit. It's healthy and so she goes back to work, as usual."

He paused for a moment. "She still sleeps outside, though, until she gets permission from the tribe."

He looked along a nearby track which wandered down to the lake. A party of the day's hunters was coming towards them.

"Looks as though we shall be feeding soon. Couple of large beaver!"

The Chief was among them. He approached Peter and placed a hand on his arm.

"The weather is changing towards Spring, my friend.

It will be time for us to return to your new post within a few moons. If you wish to stay with us, we should welcome it. You have brought good luck".

He smiled, turned abruptly and walked away.

Peter consulted his journal. It was the end of March and so he estimated that, all things being equal, they would arrive at Malcolm Ross's House sometime during early April.

"I must say that I'm delighted with young Fidler" Turnor said to Ross.

"Yes. We can be very proud of him. He's a very fit hand for the

Company. He stands hunger and can eat anything the Indians will".

The fire crumpled in its centre and Ross placed a couple more logs on it.

"Now that he's returned, I think he can have a rest for a couple of weeks, then we'll return to Cumberland House".

"A couple of weeks, hey! I can use him during that period. After that, I think he'll be glad to be back on the trail again, don't you?"

The two men laughed.

Turnor was relaxed in a large chair cut out of one piece of wood. Ross was sitting on an upturned box, leaning his back against the sturdy table leg.

"You'll need to take plenty of provisions, Philip. My Indians say that game is very scarce"

"And I'm sure they are right. I'm hoping that Roderick McKenzie is still there. I think he'll treat us right"

"Maybe so, Philip, maybe so. But I never trust those Northwesters!"

Turnor knew the story of Malcolm's cousin John and remained silent.

"The reason I'm going at all, Malcolm, between you and me, is that I have to get to York Factory in time to catch a ship to London."

Ross looked surprised but said nothing.

"I have to make my report to the Committee. If there is anything I can do for you, let me know and consider it done"

"Why. Thank you Philip. That will be worth thinking about."

"I'll take Peter with me, Malcolm as far as York House. I need his maps as I need yours to take to London with me. I believe it will be seen that they are a major contribution towards understanding the geography of northwestern Ruperts Land."

He looked at the neat pile of documents laid out on the table.

"These cover the details of the route from York Factory to Cumberland House and then across to Lake Athabasca and Great Slave Lake.

I estimate that it's a route sixteen hundred miles long giving access to the Arctic. We've established without doubt the exact geographical position of Chipewyan post and Lake Athabasca. Our predecessors, Samuel Hearne and Peter Pond and even Alexander MacKenzie have guessed those places miles out of place and many degrees west of their actual positions. We know exactly where they lay and their exact positions relative to Fort Churchill"

61

He paused, but went on excitedly.

"The western edge of British Columbia has been plotted by Captain Cook, so we know exactly the distance from here to the sea. It's a lot further than either Pond or McKenzie dreamed!"

Ross savaged a broken nail with his front teeth.

"I don't think Chief Tomison attaches as much importance to it as that, Philip. He's a very old fashioned, stubborn man, in my opinion. I don't ask you to agree, but that's my opinion!"

"I wouldn't put it quite as strongly as that, Malcolm, but I think that Mr Colen at York Factory is of a similar mind. And if they are not careful, the pair of them may find themselves in conflict between the Committee's needs and their own impressions.

"If there is a serious difference of opinion, Philip, young Thompson and Fidler, not to mention me, won't know which way to jump, and that's for sure!"

He savaged the broken nail again and spat into a spittoon.

"Part of my remit is still to take Thorburn to Thorburn's Rapids and establish a post there. I may do that during the fall"

He paused and examined the calloused finger which oozed a spot of blood.

"Of course" he said "Thompson took the last furs north to York Factory and he's been there ever since. He's fit enough now, I think, so I'm expecting him here any time" He paused.

"He's a good lad and very ambitious. Did you know about his letter from the Committee?".

"Letter? To him personally? No, I didn't!"

"Yes. Commendation when he finished his apprenticeship. He's a bit younger than Peter but he's been in service longer since they recruited him from Grey Coat School. Made him a present of some mathematical instruments, I understand. Brass compass, thermometer and some other stuff. Nice Hey?"

Turnor grunted but made no reply.

He stood with his back to the fire, hands on thighs, deep in thought.

"I'm going to have to send young Fidler out again" he said. "To contact the Piegans"

Ross sat bolt upright

"The Plains Tribes! I know they come in now and again, but we've sent very few people to them before. They are very unsociable! Very dangerous!"

"Turnor nodded.

"What you say is true, I'm sure, Malcolm. However, I'm inclined to think that they are very suspicions of us at the moment. Nowadays, they have to come to us instead of us going to them. I think they are used to our people travelling with them, including, I might add, young Thompson in '87 with James Gady.   Long before that, probably forty years ago, Anthony Henday did the same ." He hesitated and rocked on his heels.

"So we are not exactly breaking new ground, are we? Just reconsolidating old ground"

"But what is the advantage to us, Philip?"

"Furs, economics, territorial expansion, geographical knowledge, discovery of places and substances useful to us and unknown to the Indians. A great deal of what we treat as superfluous rubbish is of great value to the Indians who are still in the stone age. They use brittle bones and sharp thorns for sewing and many Indian womens' lives are full of such chores. They will trade piles of unwanted furs for some steel needles. Take fires for example. When they move, a steady, careful old man carries a rough wooden bowl holding earth and the embers of their fire. A single fire is made and one from each tent fetches some for their own. Imaging the reduction in trouble and anxiety when they are given flints for which they will exchange their finest wolf or beaver skins. The trade is not just one way, Malcolm, as you well know".

Ross had remained silent during Turnor's small speech and watched his boss closely.

He nodded at the end of it.

"Of course, you are quite right, Philip. I knew all this, but I haven't sat and thought about it like you."

"I particularly want Fidler to make observations of the Rocky Mountains" said Philip. "I'd like to get them on our maps as soon and as accurately as possible. There should be no trouble about his skill. He's a fully-fledged surveyor, now and a good linguist to boot. If anyone can learn from the Blackfeet Indians, it'll be him!"

"I understand that he's inherited some property in England?"

"I believe so, but he doesn't talk much about it. It's at a place called Bolsover, in Derbyshire, not an area that I know. But he hasn't shown any interest in running back there. He likes what he's doing here. Thank God!"

They both smiled and nodded.

CHAPTER 4

Buffalo Hunters

(1792 - 1793)

Peter Fidler's ears were burning. He rubbed them, moved the oil lamp slightly to get a better view of an invoice open on the desk alongside a heavy ledger.

"I think somebody must be talking about me, as my old Gran told me. Ears burning" he said.

His colleague, John Ward, sat opposite him.

"Dunno about ears, but that band of Piegans we are about to be lumbered with are a miserable looking lot."

Ward didn't seem to be the sort of man that would be upset by anything. Suntanned, stocky, clad in fringed leathers, he was the epitome of a backwoodsman.

A Buffalo (Bison) Jump or Pound
Native American hunters driving a herd of buffalo over the edge of a cliff. Young men will kill all that survived, so that none escapes, then women butcher the remainder.

Cocking his head and looking at Peter's entries he grunted,

"I reckon we are going to need a horse each to ride and another one each to carry that stuff!"

Peter was still thinking about Ward's first remark.

"Yes. You're right, John. They aren't very happy, are they!. I suppose it's because they arrived at the fort with little to trade and so they've got nothing back. However, we may be able to save their face and do the Company a bit of good by taking this stuff to their encampment"

He turned the heavy ledger round for Ward to read.

Ward looked uncomfortable and said "No. No. That's alright, Peter. You read it out to me"

"OK. This is the stuff which should pay for our board over the winter and for us to give as occasional presents.

Tobacco, roll, 17 pounds, Tobacco, Brazil, 92 pounds, Vermilion 4 ounces, Flints 40, Beads, large, 10 pounds, Powder, 12 pounds, Ball, 7 pounds, Shot, Bristol, 7 pounds, Worm gun, 2 , Steels, fir, 4"

He turned over the foolscap page and continued the list.

"Beads, common, 4 pounds, Beads, China, 2/3 of a pound, Knives, woman's.24,   Knives, Yew handle 12,

Knives, pocket 2, Hatchets, Oval eye 2, File 2, Bayonets, large, flat, 2, and finally, Kettle, 2 gallon size."

"So the day after tomorrow is still on, is it?"

"Yep. About two o'clock in the afternoon. That's the 8th November, so while I'm about it, I'll head up my journal"

He lifted his journal from the end of the table and opened it in front of him.

Licking the end of a quill pen, he wrote in a large, flowing hand and spoke out loud as he did so.

"Journal of a Journey overland from Buckingham House to the Rocky Mountains in 1792 and 1793, by Peter Fidler"

"This is going to be a wintering further south than anybody has been so far. Should you put that?"

"I've thought about it, John, but I think that will come out as we go along. I'll record all my observations, latitude and longitudes etcetera, so it will soon become clear if that is the case"

"Fine, Peter. I'll bring the horse round and hope to be away by eight. Is that all right?"

"Fine, John. Gives us time to get a bit of shuteye tonight." He stood up, stretched upwards and yawned.

"So, I'll see you with the horses. Good night John"

"What time do you reckon it is, John?"

"My calculations make it about 2 in the afternoon, Peter and we should be near the river crossing soon". He looked around at their companions, the Chief, his wife and another Piegan.

"At least we should have les snow when we ford it. My horse is not very happy with this deep snow. The Chief's horse and his wife's seem to be coping all right."

"When we have crossed the river, I think we should make a large fire and warm the horses" said Peter, urging his horse into the water.

Afterwards, they rode up the long slope southerly and pitched camp about five miles from the river.

They slept well and rose early, but had to spend time rounding up the horses.

Peter entered details about Landon Lake and their course took then sixteen miles to the south west.

"Unless I'm mistaken, I think we've caught up with one tent of those who left Buckingham House before we did."

"I'm not surprised " said John."This land is a morass of small lakes and only small clumps of aspen and willow."

"I think we'll call it 'Derwent' "decided Peter.

The next day was mild and they crossed another river which Peter marked as the 'Vermilion' River. He noted in his journal that on both sides were fine, open grass lands. Unfortunately, a fire had swept the area, so it was difficult to feed the horses.

"Some of those up front seem to be in a hurry" observed John.

"I think they are in a hurry to get home. They've been away some time".

He thought a moment as their horses gathered speed.

"I believe they said that they lived by the Red Deer River. As well as that, the Snake and Kootenay people have made peace with our Piegan Muddy River tribe after a lot of bloodshed. The Chief wants to meet them. I think he wants to show us off!" he nodded ahead. "There's an encampment on the horizon, John. Not all Piegans either"

The newcomers were three tents of Crees alongside fourteen tents of Piegans.

"It makes me smile to see the way the braves behave" said John. "They never walk if they can ride. This group has been living on bull buffalo meat. They couldn't find any cows".

"Have you seen that dense cloud along the horizon, John ?" asked Peter, shading his eves and peering towards the west.

"Yep. Thought they might have a storm over there"

"Well. Hold on to your hat, 'cos I think they are the Rocky Mountains and if they are, then it's the first time I've seen them"

The Indians who had hurried to this camp had become reunited with their friends and families. They were in no mood to move.

"They still haven't found any cows" commented John.

"I have to bite my tongue" said Peter " The fur trader in me wants them to trap instead of hunt!"

Peter, with John's assistance, continue taking observations regularly.

He fixed on the Devil's Head mountain as they drew nearer to the Rocky Mountains.

"What have they done to the dogs!" queried John in surprise.

Peter examined a couple standing dejectedly nearby. They had bundles of dry wood and buffalo dung tied to their backs.

The Buffalo Jumps

They past the point known as Lone Pine and entered the treeless plains to the south, camping near Rosebud Creek, blessed with flowing springs.

On 5th December, the party headed towards the top of a high rock on the end of the Creek. On either side of them, stretching in a 'V' to the distance, were waist high piles of buffalo dung at thirty yards intervals.

"This must be the buffalo pounds or jumps that we've heard of" said Peter excitedly and rode to the edge of the 40 foot drop.

"See there!" he said pointing "They drive them in this vee shape and they crowd together and can't see what's in front. Especially as they'll be running and those ahead will be churning up dust! Then, wham! They are over the edge."

A pungent odour of decay rose from below. Skulls and large bones were in evidence.

Their vocabulary was improving and they were able to understand the Chief's description of the pound.

"Men and boys drive herd. Women wait . They kill buffalo. Kill all buffalo. None must escape. Stop their spirits telling others. Women then butcher animals. "

On another occasion he said "Always start day of hunt with smoking and prayers to Great Spirit, Manitou and other gods.

"They sometimes chase a herd for forty miles, running all day on foot. Only the young, fit men can do that," explained Peter, as he entered details in his journal.

"One of the braves told me that his mother had been killed at a hunt about a year ago" said John. "A buffalo fell on her from above. " He paused.

"I didn't dare ask him what she was doing underneath a mountain, pouring with huge buffalo!"

"Any way, if they kill less than fifty at one go, it's considered very small. And they only cut small pieces off their kill. Tongues and testicles being the main delicacies. Do you know why they keep mentioning the lack of cow buffalo?"

"Go on " said Peter.

"It's because they kill those in calf and they particularly like to eat the developing calves which have hair on them."

Peter spent some time counting the buffalo remains.

"I reckon there is an enormous amount of wastage, John. There must be 250 carcasses in that pound over there!".

As they left the encampment, pressing on into the prairies, braves hunted buffalo with bow and arrow.

Mostly, they killed the animal with one shot, but where they missed the heart, they would ride alongside, lean over and remove the arrow to use it again and kill the beast. Sometimes, arrows would travel clean through the animal without touching a bone.

Arrows were shod with pieces of iron, such as old kettles, battered and shaped between two stones.

Put On Show

One of the Piegans approached John and Peter. Without change of expression he said

"You. Both. Good thing put on best clothes. Clean up."

"Of course" said Peter " Is there any reason such a request?"

"Apart from the obvious, that we smell like skunks!" muttered John.

The brave remained blank. He started to walk away then changed his mind.

"Snake Indian visit camp. Chief wants him see you".

He spun on his heel and stalked away, duty done.

"This Snake Chief is very important to us" said Peter's Chief.

The Snake eyed Peter and John up and down then stepped forward suddenly. He unfolded his arms and with one hand, pinched Peter's cheek. Peter stood perfectly still. The Chief leaned forward and looked into Peter's eyes.

"He is very astonished at the colour of your skin and eyes and hair" said Peter's Chief proudly.

The Snake stepped back and spoke.

"He is inviting us to smoke a peace pipe" said the Piegan Chief.

Peter took out his magnifying glass and tilted the pipe bowl towards the bright sunlight. Within seconds, the tobacco burst into flames and the Snake Chief leapt away as though stung, indicating that he wanted to be well away from such magic.

The Piegans were delighted at the Snake's discomfiture and his astonishment at these,

"We are the first white men he has ever seen. Our hosts have gained importance by being acquainted with magical white men", said John barely able to keep a straight face.

"There's more than just the one Snake" said John next morning. "There's about three or four, as far as I can reckon. They seem to be finishing a peace treaty that's been made. "

"There's some trouble with that lad over there" replied Peter."I can't make out whether he's one of ours or one of theirs, although he looks a bit different than both!"

"As far as I can understand it, Peter, he's a Flathead. Caught trying to steal our horses. Some of our lot want to put him to death, but the Chief has said 'no!'"

"That's a surprise!. They normally aren't as humane or lenient as that! He's got off lightly"

Peter mentioned the matter to the Chief that evening who was not very pleased that the white men were concerned with tribal business.

"I intend to reprimand him severely and send him home." he said. "His parents will be glad to see him as I would be glad to see mine. Also, it is good tribal business. We are trying to form peace treaties with all the tribes around us. This will produce friendship and consideration instead of a war for revenge."

He wrapped his blanket closer around himself and continued.

"Tomorrow, we reach our land, one favoured by Manitou. We shall be plenty people."

Into Blessed Country

And they were. Seven hundred tents awaited them in High River, a blessed land, swept by the gentle Chinook winds which dropped down the mountain face and swept away the snow.

"They never seem to resent you asking them questions" observed John as Peter updated his journal.

"You'll probably have the most up-to-date record of the modern Piegan and Plains Indians as anybody ever has!"

Peter smiled wryly and grunted, concentrating his entries.

"They've got another two herds ready for two more jumps" said John. "They kill an awful lot of buffalo, but the critters keep on comin'".

"I was just writing about that" said Peter, rubbing the side of his face absently with the goose quill. He looked at the feather as though he had never seen it before, then said

"They bring us 8 or 10 buffalo, but it's only about the same as a goose at Hudson's Bay! Anyway, I 'd planned that we go to "The Old Woman's Buffalo Jump" tomorrow if that's all right with you?"

John nodded. "Fine by me. I understand that they've been using this for many years. The Chief's version was either ten hundred or ten thousand years, I couldn't work out which one!"

John looked over Peter's shoulder and he mouthed the words "Squaw Coulee".

"I remember hearing something about that " he said, musingly."Long time before this trip, though. Remind me about it, will you"

"Well, the Great Spirit, or the Old Man as they sometimes call him, made everything, including men and women. But his sense of humour had him put the women together at Squaw Coulee and the men at Boneyard Coulee. And neither knew the other existed. Until, that is, one of the women was hunting far afield and she met a man doing the same. They stopped to talk and smoke and fathomed out what the Old Man had done!. So that night, the men all moved into Squaw Coulee.!"

"A good yarn!" laughed John.

"The old man who told me thought it was. He wrinkled with merriment when he told me that it was 'the beginning of things!'"

Just after Christmas, several young men came, bringing 25 good horses they had stolen from the Snake Indians, irrespective of the fact that a peace treaty had been made. They passed a message to the Chief that a number of Kootenay Indians were waiting to barter horses for our goods.

The Chief reminded Peter and John that the Kootenay had never seen white men before and tried to persuade the explorers not to go. When Peter was adamant, the Chief informed them that thirty of his men would keep an eye on them both at all times!.

The men walked to the trading spot carrying hatchets, kettles, beads which they hoped to trade for horses.

It lay in the shadow of Chief Mountain, venerated by Cree and Blackfoot alike.

Unknown to all at that time, the mountain was across the boundary in the United States and they were at the USA /Canada border.

They met the Kootenay Chief, who greeted them with a kiss and with twelve of his men, they travelled to a place long known as 'Old Mans Bowling Green'.

It was an arena some 30 yards long and 10 yards wide used as the court for an Indian game. Peter wrote the details in his journal, the first white man to have seen the sport.

The space was surrounded by piles of stones on which referees sat. Players rolled a 4 inch hoop and others threw arrows by hand to pass through them. Those who did so whilst the hoop was rolling were considered to have won The Chief had an explanation for its origins.

"Many ages ago, white man, with white hair, came from South. He arranged for all local tribes to play this came in competition instead of fighting each other. The same man made buffalo for Indians."

"Have you seen what our men get for their wares?" asked John.

"They are able to trade old kettles and hatchets for horses!"

Peter sneaked way whilst his watchers were busy   bartering. He climbed Thunder Mountain and took bearings of the Rockies from Kicking Horse Pass towards Central Montana.

He was met in a cloud of dust by mounted Piegans.

"We nearly went to war with the Kootenay" said their leader testily. "We were sure that they had disposed of you!"

The Kootenay Chief was quite talkative.

"We live over the mountains towards the Great Salt Ocean" he told Peter."No buffalo that side of mountains. No white men traders that side of mountains. Every time we try to visit white man trade settlements, we are stopped".

"Stopped? Who by?" asked Peter in puzzlement.

The Chief hesitated briefly, then swept his arm around.

"Muddy River tribe, Blood tribe, Black Feet, Southern Indians. All stop my people."

"I reckon" said Peter " that there's about 30 different nations I've counted so far, and they speak about 15 different and distinct languages."

He walked about their tent, crouching slightly, with arms tucked under his armpits.

"When I get time, after this, I'm going to collect them together into a book"

The Medicine Man

A few days later, when the Kootenays were preparing to leave, a band of Crees arrived.

"The Chief said that they are welcome because they are great doctors" said John. "I notice that they trade roots, leaves and stuff that they've gathered, for skins" He snorted.

"I reckon they are just too lazy to hunt for themselves and they've found a way of getting someone else to do the dirty work!"

The Crees soon noticed the white men and traded their newly acquired skins for tobacco and ammunition.

"Our Piegan Muddy River Indians are not very pleased" commented Peter "They think that they have an exclusive right to everything we trade. Mind you, they do purchase our stuff fairly"

"I remember that Anthony Henday some years ago reckoned that the Plains Crees acted as middle men in a number of ways. Selling medicine for skins is one way, but they trade for our stuff, then re-trade it at higher prices for skins to get more of our stuff!" He snorted again.

"Did you notice that the tobacco that we traded with them they have taken straight to the last of the Kootenay and added another 100 percent on the price!"

"They certainly have plenty of customers!" Said Peter, standing at the tent flap. "I've just been counting. I calculate there are about 190 of our Piegan tents, 13 Blackfeet, 12 Sarcees and four or five Plains Crees."

"I'm not surprised, Peter. There are about two thousand horses grazing on the hillsides"

He smiled.

"It always tickles me when you take your observations! The new indians come and watch the white man's magic! It's been the mildest winter for years, you know, and the Chief reckons it's because you keep scanning the skies! Some kind of relationship with the elements and the gods"

"There's a small crowd gathering around that Blood Medicine Man's tent. Let's amble over and take a look" said Peter.

The Chief and the Medicine Man were seated on ceremonial blankets and smoking. A ring of Piegans respectfully surrounded them.

"I have come to ask that you look into the spirit world and tell us what has happened to our young men."said the Chief.

He puffed and looked at the ground. The Medicine Man did the same

"Tell me about them" said the Blood suddenly, without raising his eyes.

"They went on a mission to visit our friends, the Snakes to the south. It has been several weeks and they have not yet returned. We would be grateful for news of them"

The Blood nodded slowly but said nothing.

Abruptly, he stood with arms outstretched and held the head of his pipe to four points of the compass in turn. He then stopped and said something in low tones to the Chief who gave orders to some of his men.

Peter and John eased their way to the front of the circle.

The Blood had been tied hand and foot with rawhide thongs.

Nearby, a small, special tent was erected and the Blood carried into it.

The Piegans who had carried him gathered in its doorway and others crowded all around it. No-one could get in or out.

Then there was a gasp of astonishment. The Medicine Man stooped under the tent opening and came out, completely free of his bindings.

With closed eyes and face to the South, he spoke in an unintelligible language. After a pause, he spoke out clearly in Piegan.

Three hours had passed since his meeting with the Chief who was standing next to him, listening intently.

"The young men are safe. They are returning. They will be here at the end of two more days."

chanted the Blood in a sing-song voice. He paused, swayed then went on "They have fallen lame. It has slowed them down".

He sat down suddenly, with a bump and all the spectators followed suit.

"I don't believe any of this hocus-pocus" said John scathingly. "He's only got two days to be right or wrong. He'll probably sling his hook before two days are up!"

73

The Blood stayed near his ten appearing confident in his superior knowledge and magical ability.

On the third day, the young men returned safely.

"Why were you so late" asked the Chief.

Some of the returners were limping.

"Several of our group have swollen legs through walking", replied their leader.

Peter shook his head.

"What can you say!" he said to John. "How do you explain it?"

He turned and walked with John to their tent."I don't believe in this necromancy. I think it is by chance or extra knowledge rather than by magic"

They walked together to their tent, deep in thought

"It makes you wonder, don't it!" was John's final word

Coal & Cactus

It was February and time to make the return journey to Buckingham Fort. At the end of a week when the indians had been killing cows and taking the unborn calves, they arrived at Kneehills Creek on the Red Deer River. It was 12th February 1793.

John was rinsing himself in the creek   but Peter was examining the nearby steep bank rising above them.

"What's so interesting there, Peter?""If I'm not mistaken, this is coal. Similar to that which we have in Bolsover, my home village in England. I haven't seen any like this before in any of our travels. I reckon this layer is about 15 inches thick by 60 yards long".

He stepped back and looked up, down, each side.

"Two seams. That one there" he said, pointing " is about 28 feet from the surface and the other about 34 feet"

He was the first man to record coal at Drumheller coalfield.

A little later, they lost sight of the Rockies and continued through the prairies.

Buffalo were everywhere and became denser and denser. Occasionally, they were incorporated in the fringes of huge herds.

"They spread from due north, outwards and continue due south" said Peter.

"Yep. I've tried counting them" replied John" It's impossible!"

Peter tried to assess numbers.

"They stretch as far as the eye can see in all directions. I reckon that's a good ten miles. Working that out, there must be some millions in sight! No ground can be seen anywhere"

Ten days later, when Fidler's group was still camped at Red Deer River, there were still vast herds moving towards the west. When Indians forced their way into the herds and killed the beasts, other animals merely filled the space.

They were visited by 17 young Blood Indians who came over to visit them.

Their leader said "We have just been on an expedition with a group of Snake brothers to fight the Crow Mountain Indians. We killed 35 men of that tribe . Only 3 escaped."

Peter and John found it difficult to keep their faces unemotional.

"We take Spanish guns, swords, shields, bows, arrows, clothing and scalps"

From underneath his blanket he drew 4 scalps and placed them on the ground. These were the only reward permitted them by the Snake Indians, but they thought it was enough.

Additionally, it gave some idea of the vast distances travelled by Plains Indians to conduct their forays.

It was whilst Peter was examining a cactus, his description being the first made by a white man, (Opuntia Polycantha), the Indians told them that these cactus grew to the size of large bushes along the 'Mis sis su rey' river.

"We shall be going to the trading fort tomorrow " the Chief told them. "If you wish a message to be taken, we shall take one for you"

Peter drafted a letter to Tomison at the 'Buckingham House' fort informing him they were well and would return about 20th March"

And so they did.

They descended from the hills towards the ford, passing camps of half-breed Frenchmen and then camps of Bloods.

His own Indians would not let them ride into the fort without due decorum. Young bucks were the advance party to tell the traders who was coming. The traders were then expected to make presents of tobacco. Next day, the group would arrive in proper state and be welcomed accordingly.

Peter and John parted from their friends. They had lived closely with them for 5 months and been treated with great hospitality and friendship.

CHAPTER 5

Uprising & Exploration

Tomison had built a fort at Buckingham House.

"It sure looks strong and permanent" said John Ward when it came into sight.

"Nobody seems very bothered that the North Westers' 'Fort George' stands in plain sight, some few hundreds of yards away!" commented Peter. "I understand that it is manned by Angus Shaw and his large staff."

Peter, John Ward, William Flett and Mr Thomas Thomas, a junior surgeon, had been called to a meeting with Mr Tomison.

Peter relaxed in the doorway to the trading building, gazing downstream.

"A bit of daydreaming, Peter?" asked John.

"I suppose so, John. I was watching the river flow downstream towards Manchester House, 115 miles away, then Cumberland House the headquarters for the inland trade, 500 miles and then, 700 miles beyond that is York Factory and Hudson's Bay".

"Yes Peter. This is a useful vantage point, Buckingham Fort. We can see a good three miles downstream and probably five upstream. Mr Tomison says nothing goes in or out of Fort George without we know about it."

The meeting was short and pointed. Mr Tomison was not one for fancy words or speeches.

"You will all be aware that Peter Pangman went up river from here some three years ago. Well, I understand that Mr Shaw and his North Westers are planning a similar expedition.

I intend that you will beat them to it. I believe his plan is to establish another fort upstream at the mouth of Sturgeon River which I estimate is about 200 miles up river. Peter has had words with me and he will be taking you to look the situation over. I hardly need to tell you that, if they beat us to it, they can eliminate all fur trade from that direction. That will be a disaster. You will travel on horseback, taking a spare each with you".

He looked around.

"Any questions?"

76

"It will be April 1st 1793" said John.

"Yes?" said Tomison, frowning.

"April Fools Day"

"I see. Well, let it be for the NorthWesters, not for us"

He wheeled and left.

After following Indian trails and mistakenly thinking that low clouds were the Rockies, they arrived after a week at the Sturgeon River, variously known also as the Tea River and Red Willow Creek.

Peter was not happy with the idea of a fort at Sturgeon and his group returned back towards Buckingham Fort. On the way home, they met Angus Shaw and party travelling towards the place they had recently left. Mr Shaw offered them breakfast and they parted amicably going in different directions.

Tomison was satisfied with the report. Peter and his team stayed around the fort, packing furs and making preparations to go downstream. On 13th May, 1793, Fidler aged 23 years, embarked in his canoe and with others, left Buckingham for Cumberland and then on to York Factory, where they arrived on July 4.

Two weeks later, Alexander Mackenzie reached the Pacific Ocean and inscribed his name on a rock to inform everyone that he had crossed the continent successfully.

Peter cooled his heels at York Factory and, whilst there in 1794, he met and married his life-long partner to be, 'Mary', a Cree Indian. That was not her real name, but it was Peter's mother's name. He was happy to be with her during her first pregnancy and had no great urge to leave her.

The Committee in London, however, realising that Fidler had been around the Fort for nearly two years, wrote angrily that his talent was being wasted. That he should be employed at surveying.

Tomison sent him in charge of a group to survey the Assiniboine River of northeastern Saskatchewan starting in the late summer of 1795

It was the area to which Charles Isham had been some few years before to obtain birch bark for the Company's transport system

The group met in York Factory .

"We shall leave York Factory on the 5th September and travel from Long Point Cedar Lake to Swan River House, Somerset and Carlton Houses and the upper parts of the Red River. My wife Mary and our young son, Thomas will accompany me. I have planned on 6 canoes and the

77

expedition will comprise Mr Isham, George Sutherland, John Wright, surgeon, Mr Bird, John Peter Pruden and 4 working hands in each canoe."

He looked around at the faces gathered there. All were intent on his remarks.

" We shall need to portage over the north end of Lake Winnipeg and I shall be surveying as we go. I have received some new instruments from the Committee including a 12 inch brass sextant made by Cary of London. It has an artificial mercury horizon. There is also a watch with hand, made by J. Jolly of London. A very good one, too. Please feel free to look at them on the table".

He looked around again.

"There will be some places of interest along the route. During the portage we shall see the grave of a long-dead Southern Indian Chief who was buried over 70 years ago. You'll see that every Indian who passes here gathers up a lump of moss and throws it upon his grave as a mark of respect. He was said to be very old and on his way to Hudson's Bay when he died..

Another place of interest is likely to be the Canadian House built by Mr Cuthbert Grant, which I understand is still inhabited. It should be about 12 miles up the Swan River".

The party left as scheduled, examined the places Peter had mentioned and moved on to Swan River House a few hundred yard from Cuthbert Grant's House.

It was occupied by Mr Hallett, a Company employee and John Johnston Jr who had a bad thumb!

"I understand that Mr Isham built this house" said Peter to Mr Hallett.

"Yes. That's right. 1790 it was. At that time this was the most northerly situation in which oak was reported to grow".

He hesitated briefly.

"Incidentally, I think it should be known that we are feeling the pinch from a new house the Northwesters have built further up the Assiniboine River. The principal part of the Indian trade has gone there"

"Perhaps you would like to accompany me into that area" suggested Peter "You me and Mr Isham can journey there by horse. We only have three available for carrying trading stores and goods. However, I think we may be able to borrow or buy some extra from the local Indians. We will take eight men to build a Company post if feasible"

He sipped at a mug of sweet tea.

"How do you acquire sugar?" he asked.

Hallett smile with pleasure."It isn't sugar as we know it, Peter. No. It's one that the trappers and Indians tap from the local maple trees. It's their sap. Very tasty, too!"

The North West Company men were building Fort Alexandria when Fidler and his group arrived on 22nd October 1795.

He immediately sought out a site about 15 miles away and they began building Carlton House, 26 feet long and 22 feet wide.

It was discovered that there were a number of trading posts established throughout the area, not only Northwesters, but independents also. The Plains Crees and Assiniboine Indians took advantage of the rivalries.

"We've had a comfortable winter" Peter told Isham."I'm required to spend the summer in charge of Cumberland House."

"It's become a most important post at the crossroads of the fur trade" observed Isham. "As well as furs, almost all our supplies of pemmican and stores come through there, nowadays. You have been given an important assignment, Peter."

"I think that is so, Charles. I am happy that it allows me to keep in contact with old friends and colleagues. Walker, Hudson, Bird, Oman, Flett, Gaddy, Hallett, and last but not least, David Thompson."

He poured more maple syrup into his tea and stirred it.

"It also gives you the opportunity to travel into the prairies again. You have a lot of friends among the Indians there, Assiniboine, Piegans, Blackfeet, Bloods, Sarcees, Gros Ventres. Not many people know them as well as you or speak the language!"

Peter nodded.

"It will give me a great deal of pleasure to remake old acquaintants. Afterwards, I think that I'm scheduled for Buckingham House under the general command of George Sutherland, the new Inland Master. I don't know how long I shall remain there, but it will give Mary a chance to settle down for a while"

During the past year, trouble had arisen with the Gros Ventres Indians who reasoned that the white men were allies of their enemies.

Soon, the Indians attacked Europeans in order to wrest firearms from them by force.

Following an attack on the Northwester Fort of Pine Island where they were beaten off, the next target was adjacent Hudson's Bay's Manchester

House, guarded by only four men. They disarmed the men and sacked the post.

Both Forts were abandoned some months later in favour of Buckingham House and their demise left a deep impression on all traders.

There were many comings and goings between the major houses, involving Tomison, Thompson, James Davey, Magnus Annals, William Fea, Hugh Brough and others.

Tomison maintained thirty nine men at Buckingham whilst the Northwesters had eighty men at Fort George just a gunshot away. The total numbers when swelled by women and children would be double those numbers.

Mr Tomison went to Buckingham House, leaving Magnus Anbnal, Mr Vandriel, James Gaddy, William Fea and Hugh Brough at South Branch House.

At about noon on Thursday, a horseman tumbled from his horse at the front door of Hudson's Bay post. Two arrow shafts protruded from his right calf muscles.

Willing hands took him inside where he gave his name as Du Bois from the North Westers' Fort.

"I 'ave been attack by Gros Ventres twelve miles down the trail" he said with gritted teeth as they cut out the arrow heads.

"There must be a hundred of them on the warpath." He writhed in agony but made no sound. Sweat poured from his head and body and he brushed away a suggestion of a leather grip in his teeth.

"Non. Must talk. They come this way. I must warn my Fort"

No sooner was the wound bound than he had hobbled away with a crutch, mounted his horse and prepared to ride away. "They will be here within a couple of hours. Leave here and go to our Fort. Good luck"

He swung the horse's head and galloped away.

The Northwesters fort was across the river, but unable to offer Hudson's Bay any assistance in the event of an attack.

The Gros Ventres, numbering about 100, attacked the Northwesters first, but with foresight and good luck, they were repulsed by a small force consisting of 4 Canadians and 5 Cree Indians.

Angrily, the natives attacked the Hudson Bay fort, whose men were not so fortunate.

The Company had felt it unnecessary to build any defensive fortifications so that they were vulnerable to attack.

Vandriel, Fea and a few Indian men and women were there to defend it, but did not do so with any resolution.

That same night, Vandriel crept into the NorthWesters Fort, wounded but not critically.

"They killed every man, woman and child with the exception of me." he said, tears running onto his chest.. "I don't know how I escaped. It was a miracle."

Flames from the Hudson's Bay post could be seen clearly as it burned to the ground.

One of the Crees had followed the attacker's progress from a distance.

"They took loot and retired to prairie. They go in two groups. One group go South. Other go to join Snake Indians."

Their rage was over and they vanished into the prairie night

Shortly after Fidler arrived at Buckingham, Sutherland confided his views about the need for boats.

"I would like several York boats built and sent to Edmonton House" he said.

"I have one boat built already" Peter assured him. "The boat builder and his mates are working on others"

"I feel that we need a fleet of York boats, Peter, which are ideal for the kind of waters that we are dealing with. We are doing very good business with our suppliers. My only concern is the shortage of goods. John Pruden and I have six men with us and a number of horses to take goods from here to Edmonton House. I trust the weather will hold off."

It didn't.

Sutherland returned through the blizzards having lost most of the horses to the cold.

"Rest a few days and see if the weather improves" said Peter. "I can supply you with dog teams"

"I came through the tents of a lot of Stone Indians" said Sutherland."It was our hope that they would deal with Edmonton, rather than here and we would like to encourage the Blackfeet to trade at Buckingham"

"The problem is" said Peter "We are having trouble persuading the Blackfeet to come here. Most of what they bring is prairie furs, buffalo, wolves and other stuff low in value and I know you've turned them away from Edmonton, but they say they are afraid to come here because there are so many Stones."

81

"They've told me that it will change in the spring" said Sutherland. "They are talking about making war with the Stones. I don't care who kills who, but warring Indians and particularly dead ones, don't trap furs!"

I agree . By the way, have you noticed the increase in comings-and-goings of Mohawks recently? And a few Iroquois? They are both trapping beaver. I'm told that the Mohawks have even trapped across the Rockies in Oregon! Most of their trade is with Fort George but we've had a few visits from them. At least they don't seem worried about Stones or Gros Ventres!"

Sutherland examined his own weather beaten clothes.

"How are the new coats coming along? " he said suddenly.

"Fine. George. Fine. The tailor told me this morning that he's finished 16 small Indian coats and cut out 7 Captains' Coats of Aurora cloth with 3 of them in a fine blue".

"Well, down to business Peter. I want to abandon Buckingham House for the summer. Just for the summer mind you. I would take it kindly if you would arrange for all the horses to be loaded with provisions and send them along the river bank to Edmonton along the south side of the river. It's the trail that's been used several times before and with relations cordial between ourselves, the Northwesters and Indians, it should be a good time to make the transfer."

"What will happen to the House then, George?"

"Mr Shaw from the Canadian Fort will keep an eye on it for us, he says. I don't think there's enough trade for both of us during the summer anyway, so we shall be better off in Edmonton than here."

"You want me to go to Edmonton?"

"No, Peter. I want you to take all the remaining canoes and York boats down to the Bay. When can you do it?"

"Well. That will be 19 canoes and two boats. So, I think towards the end of May would be a reasonable assessment"

"I expect Mr Tomison to pass through here some time in October on the way to Edmonton, after his trip to England.

I'll move down to take over about November. After the Bay, you can return and take over Cumberland House."

He hesitated briefly.

"I don't want to be the fly in the ointment, Peter, but I expect you've heard about David Thompson?"

"David? I hope he's all right. Nothing happened?"

"No. Not illness or anything like that. No. But did you know he's thinking of leaving us?"

Peter was surprised.

"Leaving us? Going back to England?"

"Not that either! No. He's been offered a position as Surveyor with the Northwesters and he's taking it. He's been asked to supervise the building of a fort for them at Lac La Biche. We've thought about doing the same thing for some time, but I don't know whether he's using our idea or theirs!"

Peter was still flabbergasted at the news.

"I can hardly believe it! I still think of him as my friend David, even though we meet infrequently. I've kept abreast of all his comings and goings whenever possible. But, joining the Northwesters!"

"Well, you'll like this bit even less, Peter. Your next bit of exploration has been determined already. It will occupy you during the fall of next year until the first half of 1800. In fact, your next couple of years have been mapped out.

Mapping out the work of the Mapper, hey!"

They both laughed.

"The Company wants you to be the one to survey Lac La Biche with a view to establishing our own post"

He stood and stretched luxuriously.

"So you'll go to York Factory with the canoes and boats, return to Cumberland House, spend the rest of '97 and '98 there, then off you'll go to Beaver River and Lac La Biche.

I shall be moving in the morning and it seems as though we won't be in direct touch for a while, so here's my hand, Peter. All the very best to you and your family"

They shook hands, solemnly.

CHAPTER 6

Building Bolsover House

(1799 - 1800)

"I would say that life is comfortable, wouldn't you Mary?"

Peter sat on a shaped log, racoon cap tipped over his eyes. His bare feet dangled in the lake and he was holding loosely on to a fishing rod. Mary, pregnant again, was playing with two of her children some yards from the bank and she smiled contentedly.

"I was a little scared when Roderick MackKenzie visited, husband. When he returned the meat they had borrowed I was surprised."

"I know exactly what you mean, love. We don't get on particularly well with Northwesters, but we do tend to look after one another"

They both remained silent. Then Peter s aid "I think this is better than Cumberland House. At least I can do some fishing for pleasure instead of necessity. There are supposed to be lots of sturgeon in these waters. Oh! Oh!"

He cried out as the rod was dragged through his fingers.

"I've got a bite! I bet it's a sturgeon!"

Mary stood and ran towards him. He wrestled with the rod, shortening and lengthening the pull.

"It's a big one, whatever it is!"

Then it appeared. It's whiskers bristled and it seemed to stare straight at him.

"A catfish! " said Mary. " A big one too. That will look nice in the pot".

He played it on to the bank and Mary, standing in the shallows, grabbed it. It twisted and turned but could not escape. With a flick of her strong arms, she struck the fish against a nearby tree and it sagged limply.

Together, they calculated its size.

"I make it 2 feet seven inches longs" said Peter. "That's the first catfish I've ever caught!"

"Have a look at this, Mr Fidler" called one of the men.

It was the arrival of William McGillivray with 6 canoes filled with bales of good beaver.

"Comes from Slave Lake, by the looks of 'em" said the man.

"Probably from Portage La Loche" said Peter.

"We hears as' 'ow another company is being formed to join in the ruckus" commented the man, spitting into the roadway.

"So we're told" said Peter. "I think it is to be called 'The Little Company', with Mr Richardson and Mr Ogilvie in charge."

"We heered as Alex MacKenzie was breaking with the Northwesters and joining these ' Potties' ".

"I've heard the same story, Robert ". Said Peter. "I suppose we'd better be more polite now that he's Sir Alexander MacKenzie!"

"Yep. I suppose that's right, Mr Fidler. We can't altogether trust 'em but we sometimes relies on 'em"

He paused. "I suppose you knows that Mr McTavish and your old mate, Mr David Thompson is over there at the Canadian Fort. 'Tommo' is going as master of a settlement up the Beaver River'"

Peter said nothing. A number of David's explorations, though pressed hard had bogged down.

"'E's not much of a master, Mr Fidler, with respect" said Robert. "My view is that the Company did well by 'im but he deserted 'em. He's not very good at gettin' things done!"

Peter looked angry. "I might remind you Robert that Mr Thompson was the first white man to make the Athabasca trip, which was very difficult, but he carried it through and found a route, nor shall I be happy to hear adverse comments about a brave and resourceful man, a great geographer and fine surveyor, In addition, he is my friend!"

He swung round on his heel, leaving behind a discomfitted Robert.

His second son, Charles was born at 35 minutes past noon on 10th October 1798.

He held Mary in his arms and kissed her black, shining hair.

"It will be a long journey, darling" he murmured in her ear. "The boys will be a burden, but if you are determined to come with me and bring them, then I am very happy"

"When shall we be leaving Peter?" she asked quietly.

"Next week. The 5th of August. I have no idea how long we shall be away. I have to arrange for a fort to be built at Barren Ground Lake, also known as Meadow Lake"

He looked down at her lovely face and smiled.

"We shan't be doing this on our own. It's a concentrated effort by the Company to try and win back some of the ground we've lost to the Canadians."

He smoothed her hair.

"The Churchill and Beaver Rivers will almost be overrun by our people. William Linklater is going to build at Ile-a-la-Crosse, and at Churchill Lake, William Auld is to build at Green Lake and Waterhen Lake.. The opposition is doing similar things, I understand"

"Who will be the guide for Mr Auld?" asked Mary.

"That's a good point, love. I think we'll arrange to wait for him at the southern end of Ile-a-la-Crosse. He will be using heavy boats, whilst we shall be in canoes. He carries much more than us, but is more cumbersome."

"You may have to look after your pilot more closely" said Mary. "I have it on good authority that Mr McTavish of the old Northwesters is determined to use every method, good or bad, to persuade our pilot to leave us. It could be dangerous"

Peter nodded, unsmilingly, then clasped her to him without speaking.

"Also" she said, her face almost lost in his clothes, "One of their canoes with 2 men has gone to Green Lake. It will be to tell the master there of our approach and try to drive away my people before we get there, if possible".

"It is an area where there was considerable smallpox in 1781, so I'm not sure what the numbers will be, Mary. Thankfully, that epidemic seems to be over now".

They met Auld and went to Green Lake, so called because of the amount of green floating grass. After leaving him, Peter's group went down the Beaver River till they reached Meadow Lake River on 30th August. It was swampy, twisting and shallow for much of its length. The lake itself was so shallow that he had to unload the canoes to half weight and make more than one journey.

The journey was a nightmare.

"Goddamn those sons-a-bitches" spat O'Leary as occasional shots were fired from the undergrowth. Howls, shrieks and groans frightened game and men alike.

Logs appeared out of nowhere to threaten the canoes. The 'Canadians' continued their harassment.

The pilot came to discuss matters with Peter.

"Men not very happy" he said.

Peter nodded understandingly, not needing to ask for any reasons.

"Do you have any suggestions, Joe?"

The pilot was silent for several seconds.

"You have keg of liquor. I give to men. They stay"

"I have a 3 quart keg, Joe and you can have it with pleasure, but go easy with it. All right?"

Joe nodded. "Men will hunt very well and so will locals".

He turned, as though to leave, but stopped and spoke over his left shoulder

"White man with one of my people arrives tomorrow morning about sun-up. 3 horses. Carry letters. "

Without awaiting a reply he turned and walked proudly away.

Hugh Gibson arrived next morning carrying mail, with one Indian man and three horses.

"I still don't know how they do it" said Hugh after he had been told of yesterdays prediction.

"If I believed in magic I'd swear it was magic. Except I don't!"

He went on "I'll swear that nobody could have passed us coming this way. There were no unusual signs ahead and no-one seemed to be watching us. Never even saw any smoke signals!"

Peter was opening the letters.

"One here from Mr Bird at Buckingham House. It's good to know that Henry Hallett was sent up north last September to build at Lac La Biche".

He placed the last letter on the table.

"I think I'll ask Mr Isham to accompany me with 4 men in a large canoe to go around the edge of the lake. I need to find a convenient place to settle which has both wood and water. There isn't anything suitable on the south east side and the far end of the lake."

Two days later, they returned.

"I'm not very happy with the choice" he said to Mr Isham.

"The best we can do here is those few pines about a thousand yards across the plain to the north. We can build there, but it is a long way to fetch water".

He thought for a while then said "Yes. That will do. I'm going to name the fort Bolsover House after my home town in England".

Next day, he mustered his men to give them instructions.

"We shall construct a small store, as soon as possible, about 12 feet square and get it about 5 logs high.

You'll be aware that I've paid off our pilot who did a good job"

They nodded and agreed among the cloud of smoke.

"There is plenty of buffalo about 15 miles away near Loon Lake"

"Don't think our Indians will bother them much" said a voice "They's too busy drinkin'!"

The laughter came and went. Peter noted the good spirits and even smiled at his own silent pun.

"Yes. I think you are right, Bill. Now. Down to more long term business. I'm taking some men with me in a couple of canoes, up Beaver River. I think it will be advantageous to winter with the Bungees."

A younger man looked puzzled.

Peter continued.

"The Bungees, for those who are not familiar with the term, are remnants of the Chippewa, sometimes called Saulteaux"

One man raised a hand for attention.

"Yes John?"

"Bolsover House will be finished before we go. Will anyone be staying here?".

Peter nodded. "Good question, Hugh. Yes. Mr Pruden is to come from Buckingham and take charge and you Hugh will act on my behalf until he arrives here. Is that agreeable?".

Hugh Sabeston nodded his agreement.

"I think the team basically will comprise me, William Flett, John Ballenden."

The men named nodded and remained silent.

"I know we shall need a couple more men, but I'll notify you about them later"

He stood and pointed with a walking stick at a map pinned to the wall.

"No Hudson's Bay men have ascended the Beaver River and crossed the height of land to Lac La Biche. So this will not be an easy trip. I intend to take the very minimum of pemmican and other personal provisions and live off the land"

An undercurrent of surprise circulated through the room.

"Another drawback is that we have no Indian pilot and as we have no-one who has tried this route before we don't know which is the best route."

"Haven't Hallett's men gone from Buckingham?" asked one man.

"That's true, Joe, but don't forget that they will be in front of us. We can't fetch them back to show us the route!"

There was a round of laughter. Someone trod on a dog which yelped.

"Most of what we know and what the Northwesters know is by Indian report, not by detailed survey." He paused.

"Then, last but by no means least, we have the Northwesters themselves. Angus Shaw is already planning to go out along our route and make life difficult for us. They will be taking 5 canoes I am told".

He looked sombrely around.

"We shall have to deal with these events as we come to them".

He leaned the stick against the wall.

"We shall leave early, the day after tomorrow, the 7th September".

The journey was harassed by the Canadians. Game was driven away before they could find it, leaving only tracks.

One of the men brought some objects for Peter.

"They look like fresh water clams or mussels" he said. "I'll boil some tonight in a kettle"

They were boiled as decided. The results were calamitous!

Men who had eaten them vomited into river and bushes, violently sick for a while.

Later, Fidler decided to walk along the river bank and look for spoor. There were plenty of tracks, but no sign of the animals.

He re-embarked in his canoe and when north of Loon Lake, William pointed and said quietly

"I've seen something move over there"..

"I think it's a child" said John in surprise.

They pulled into the bank and were confronted by a Canadian man, his wife and two children.

After introducing themselves, the man was asked the way to Red Deer Lake.

"I've just come from there" he said. "It will take you about four days, I reckon. I'll draw you directions"

He drew an Indian style map in the sand and marked down a number of rivers and creeks that fell into the river all the way to the lake.

Peter jotted the directions down in his rough notebook.

That evening, he said to those around the camp fire.

"I'm not very happy about these directions"

"But it's the best lead we've had so far" said William.

Others nodded and agreed.

"I hear what you are saying" said Peter "But there is something that doesn't quite fit and I'm not sure what it is at the moment".

"I think we'll pull in here" said Peter next day. "We seem to be going around in circles!"

They were at Cold Lake House which had been deserted a number of years previously.

" There's not a lot of doubt about it, lads" said Peter over a snapping, cheerful fire..

"The directions given us have turned out to be wrong and we've travelled in circles for a couple of days".

John leaned forward and lit a pipe. "It looks like we need to come up with a new idea, Peter".

A hail from the lake snapped their attention.

Fortune smiled and by accident, they had met John Irvin and Magnus Isbister on their way from Lac La Biche.

"Last people we expected to see here, guys" smiled John.

"We are on our way to Buckingham House to deliver a message. They need to know that John Richards has left us to join the Northwesters."

"I can see Angus Shaw's hand in that" added Magnus angrily,

"But at least Richards has left behind all his provisions, some of which we shall be pleased to share with you".

"Sounds like clouds and silver linings to me!" said Peter, gratefully. "I'll take some details from you about the route you've just come. We hope to find a slightly shorter route if possible"

"Lot of swamps on some routes, Peter," warned Magnus.

"And some difficult portage, but we'll be pleased to help all we can".

They parted from their colleagues at sun up and went different ways. The first day was spent working their way up the Beaver River to the height of land which would allow them to approach Lac La Biche.

John Ballenden put down his paddle.

"Can you hear somebody calling?" he asked.

"All I can hear at the moment John is 'slap', creak', 'guggle' every time I stick this paddle in the damn stream! I think I'm going to dream about it!"

90

John laughed. "Know just what you mean, Peter. But I think it came from over there" he said, pointing.

They looked closely.

Emerging from streamside bushes were three men. They wore red tartan shirts under heavy jackets, raccoon headgear, heavy boots. One waved.

John waved back. "I think they are Canadians" he said.

From twenty feet away, and after preliminary identification, the two groups conversed.

"We heard you were close in" said one of the Canadians "So we came to take you on to the new house at Greenwich".

"How far is it?" asked Peter.

""Dunno exactly, but I guess about four miles".

"Some of your guys over there" growled a very swarthy man.

"Our guys? "

"Yeah. Come from Buckingham House. Come a'build this un"

"Right. We'll follow you. Thanks" said Peter.

"Well. It's nice to be indoors. Away from the damn flies!" said John later. "Must say I was a bit nervous when those guys appeared from the bushes!"

Peter nodded without opening his eyes.

"I was just thinking" said John "We've now got two routes to the upper Athabasca. Go up the Churchill and Beaver to La Biche or from Fort George on the Saskatchewan. Mind you, you can't say either of 'em is easy."

"That's true" said Peter sleepily. "One day, ourselves and the Northwesters will want to go over the Rocky Mountains. Probably to Columbia or Oregon or both. I think this will be the likely route, unless there is another we've missed " .

"Oh! Don't say that! Don't even think about it! I've no strength left to lift even a small, toy birch-bark canoe!".

John grimaced, rolled his eyes and slumped back in his chair.

Peter flung a glove at him, playfully.

"I reckon we'll be here for the winter, John. I shan't regret that. The area is magnificent in autumn. I could stand outside and soak it up all day."

He was silent for a moment.

"D'you know, we are really beginning to open this country up. I know that we fall-out with the Canadians, but we have more in common than not in common. It's still important that we support one another. Fort George and Buckingham are only eighty miles southeast of here. Northwesters and Hudson's.

Same for Fort Augustus and Edmonton. There's a place at the mouth of the Sturgeon River that Ogilvie's have built "

He hesitated. "There are lots more but it's a bit like teaching grandma to suck eggs ! You know as well as I do!"

"I know what you mean, Peter" said John solemnly. "These little posts have increased. We tend to concentrate on beating the Northwesters, but there's the XY Company and others too.

It's a rich fur country and in eight years we've done well out of it. I didn't know whether you knew or not but your friend, David Thompson, has been working his way with three horses and twenty-five men along the Pembina River towards Lesser Slave Lake. The Canadians tell me that he's expecting to build a post there. The Beaver Indians should be good customers!"

They sat relaxed, listening to the crackle of burning wood.

"This is the time of year that I loved in England when I was a boy" Peter said suddenly. "Perhaps I'll go back to England, to Derbyshire, to Bolsover and see my mother. When we left the lake, I thought about some small ponds I used to visit in England that we called 'lakes'. Hardwick lakes, after nearby Hardwick Hall. I lay in the long grass and dreamed, watching the flocks of ducks, geese, swans on those small patches of water at home. We didn't have the numbers or variety of the ones we have here, though. Pelicans! We'd never heard of pelicans!"

He jumped to his feet.

"No point in thinking about that yet. Too much to do.

I want to get Greenwich House sorted, update all the maps for the Beaver and Athapascow rivers. There are enough packhorses for us to visit Edmonton House, which will be the next item on the agenda.

Anyway, I shall go and check that Mary and the kids are OK. See you in the morning".

With a wave, he was gone.

Winter's teeth were firmly biting the river.

Lac La Biche was frozen to the strength of steel.

Men were coming and going on the ice, carrying bundles, urging dogs, harnessing sledges.

Peter Fidler stood talking to Robert Henry, a Canadian.

"This'n 'll be your second visit to Edmonton in two months, won't it?"

Peter nodded and swung his fur mittened hands backwards and forwards.

"Should be easier this time, Rob. with the six of us on top of the water instead of in it!".

"We've had some news that your boss, Mr Bird may be coming this way early next year."

Peter refused to be surprised. "Is that so? I look forward to seeing him" was all he replied.

"And your friend, Davy Thompson is somewhere about these parts. Not sure exactly, but that's the word"

"Be pleased to see him, too. Haven't seen him for quite a while. Heard a lot, mind you. He was the first surveyor in this region

Then, slyly, "He was Hudson's Bay trained of course!"

"Heard he's seeing a lot of the Small family" said Rob.

"Patrick Small? Must confess I hadn't heard that.

Patrick Small!. Well, well. Met him many years ago on a couple of occasions. " Peter showed surprise briefly.

"It's not him he's a chasin'. It's his daughter, Charlotte. She's only thirteen or fourteen, but it sounds serious. "

"Ye Gods!. That really is interesting! I think her mother is a Cree relative of Mary!. That'd make his kids related to my kids if that's the case! I'll tell Mary. She'll work it out".

He looked around. The bustle had subsided.

"I'll have a few words with my colleagues before we leave" he said and beckoned to John Ballenden and Magnus Isbister.

Robert Henry with his two Canadians joined them out of curiosity.

"We'll be leaving within the half hour, at about 8 am.

Our route will take us past the mouth of Wandering River. Edmonton House is the reason for our journey, but I also want to establish some latitudes and longitudes. I think we are all aware that the Beaver Indians have been active in that area. They killed two men, two women and some children of the Bungees a few months ago. They may still feel like going on the warpath. It's unlikely, but we need to be aware."

He looked around at the serious faces.

"I expect to stay at Edmonton for a couple of months.

Good luck" and he walked alongside the lead sledge.

"Let's go" he said shortly.

It seemed like only yesterday that they had been on the ice waiting to move to Edmonton House.

Now, in the spring of 1800, they were travelling to Buckingham House. David Thompson had travelled the same route, two years earlier.

"That was Angus Shaw's old house, we've just passed. Built in 1790" he said to John."He lived there two or three years. So, we go towards Thin Lake River from here. I expect a water problem there and if we can't make dams, we'll have to portage, I guess"

"There are some men and horses down there" said John.

The strangers were on foot and too far away for identification.

"They aren't Indians" said Peter, suddenly.

John waved.

Two of the three men waved back and began to move closer to the water's edge.

"I do believe it's a rescue party from Buckingham House!" said John.

"Do we need rescuing then?" said Peter, smiling.

"You might not, but I do. My feet are aching at the mere thought of portaging these canoes!"

The three Hudson's Bay men shook hands all round and examined the canoes and furs.

"We've been sent to help thee take this stuff overland, Mr Fidler. Won't take a jiffy to get 'em harnessed and on our way. Leave it to me" said their leader, a stocky, red faced Englishman named George Arkwright.

"Probably a Yorkshireman" thought Peter.

"Just tell us what you want and we'll do it" he said."We're experts at canoeing, backpacking and portaging, but less so at horse-drawn methods!"

The man smiled through his long blonde beard.

"No problem. We'll be on our way before tha' can say 'Jack Robinson'"

As he turned to go he said "Incidentally, the word is that Mr Bird is on his way to the House. He's travelling quite fast from Edmonton, I'm told". He scratched his ear.

"Dunno how these folk do it! Getting the information, I mean!"

Peter nodded. "I've had the same thought on several occasions

94

Mr Arkwright. Almost magical, isn't it?".

Arkwright smiled and nodded in agreement. "Can't say as I've ever heard the drum signals, though. Used to say tha' could hear the jungle drums in Africky!" He thought briefly.

"Also heard" said Arkwright thoughtfully," that the Northwesters map-man is gonna be nearby. Over at Fort George. Chap named David Thompson? I think tha knows him".

Peter nodded, but made no reply.

"Don't suppose he'll be dropping in for tea!" said John.

Peter frowned but said nothing as he turned away.

The time to move came around again.

Mr Bird spoke to Peter about it during early May.

"Are you ready to leave, Peter?"

"Whenever you say. Any working day is long enough to get prepared. Got used to that now!"

Bird filled his prize Meerschaum pipe.

"The 18th should be fine, I reckon. I have a feeling that we shan't be using Buckingham much longer. And the Westers won't be using George, either".

He lit the pipe and drew on it with pleasure.

" There were new plans afoot before I left. Wasn't there for the final details, but it was to do with opening up the prairies"

"The prairies?" Peter was surprised. "Not a lot of business there. Lived with the Piegans for a winter. Broke even I suppose, but not a lot of furs about, except buffalo and grizzlies!"

Bird nodded.

"That's not far out, either, Peter. It's the pemmican we need.

Not much about these days to the north west. Too many competitors using it up. We need a new supply. Prairies, that's the place. You'll probably be the one chosen to go. You'll build another house. Any ideas for a name? Prairie House? Piegan House?"

"I've built Bolsover House, named after my hometown. Perhaps I'll call it Chesterfield House after the large town. nearest to Bolsover. The Crooked Spire"

" Right. So, if you'll be ready to go on the 18th, Peter, I'll join you and we can do the first part of the downstream journey together as a small fleet."

He looked around. "Feel sorry to lose the old place, but then, I always wanted to be an admiral! Runs in the family. This'll be the closest I'll ever get to it!"

He chose his next words carefully.

"Your next assignment will be very important indeed, Peter. The Company men will have to rely on you for their major food supply. The Indians are hostile. They are still fighting with each other. There are few building facilities. There may even be interference from the other companies. So, with your family commitments and long service, I wouldn't take it personally if you decided that the prairies were not for you. Don't give me an answer. I'll talk to you later at Cumberland House. All right?"

He placed a right hand affectionately on Peter's shoulder.

"I don't really have to think about it, but I understand what you are saying." replied Peter, " I look forward to discussing it later. In the meantime, I'd better make arrangements for my lot to be rolling. Or rather, sailing!"

CHAPTER 7

Indian Wars Around Chesterfield House

South Branch House a trading fort built forty miles up from the junction of Red Deer and Bad River, was as far as any white men had reached,

Business had been average with the Gros Ventres, also called 'Falls Indians' but that tribe of Indians jealously kept away all others..

Several times, small groups of 'Fall Indians' rode into the fort, empty handed and demanded liquor or guns but were refused patiently and politely.

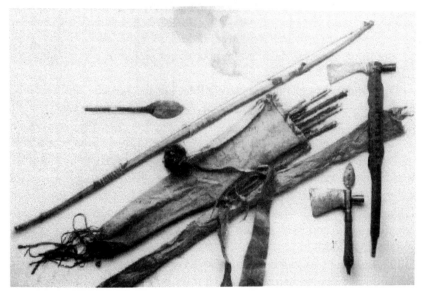

Plains Indians' weapons

Bow, quiver, arrows and axes used by Plains Indians (Plains Cree, Blackfeet of the Algonquib Tribes and others). Made mostly of wood, bone, animal hide and stone. Bows and arrows made of special kinds of wood. Arrowheads, kinives, spearheads and axes were made of chipped stone until metal became available. Quivers and bowstrings were made of strips of animal hide.

The fort settled down for the evening on 24th August, 1794.

Two dozen men, women and children lived in the House, which was poorly defended.

By eight o'clock in the evening, all were dead, doors burst open, individuals butchered and scalped in a riot of bloodshed lasting less that fifteen minutes.

The younger females were raped, then tortured for consorting with white men and hung from the edge of the log buildings. The goods were taken away, including kegs of liquor, muskets, ammunition, horses, clothes, and the place fired. The Indians rode off, whooping into the prairie darkness, lit by the roaring fires behind them.

Peter was left in no doubt why he had been chosen for this expedition.

He was resourceful, spoke Blackfoot and other languages, was familiar with their customs and known to a wide range of prairie tribes. As Bird had told him, the new mission was of the greatest importance.

Other companies, particularly the Northwesters and XY Company were planning to go into the prairies, at the same time, into the same area, for the same purpose, despite the most secret preparations by Hudson's Bay.

The availability of furs was negligible, but the buffalo herds seemed boundless. The travelling traders of North Saskatchewan needed the pemmican supply.

"So you have the complete picture, Peter." said Bird."Start 6th August, in five days. I understand that you will be approaching your site along the Red Deer and Bad River junction. That's fine with me. I'm going that far with you but you can be the admiral this time! Ably assisted by your wife, I imagine? Four boats, five canoes. We'll split at the junction and you will take two boats and twelve men. The rest will travel on with me.

Peter nodded.

"I've had reports that buffalo tracks have been seen along the way and the animals seem undisturbed, which must be a good sign!"

He looked at a map pinned to a board on the wall. It showed much greater detail than the ones he had faced some years ago.

He went on

"I've also been informed that there are canoes on the river from Edmonton. Not sure who's in them but we shall play safe. They've been travelling since 28th July so we may meet them.

They could be just as dangerous as the Indians, so I'm giving each of my men a horn of powder, 240 balls amongst them and 20 flints. I'll also make a dram of rum available to each man.

When we leave you I shall introduce a rota which ensures that every man has a loaded musket. We shall lay under arms each night, with two sentries. "

As arranged the junction, they said 'goodbye', 'safe journey' and separated.

No white man had been up this part of the journey for further than 40 miles above the old South Branch House so Peter spent much of his time in the canoe calculating distances and bearings.

He left behind a message for Pierre Belleau, a Northwesters trading master who had been identified as one of those following.

As in many instances, Fidler endeavoured to minimise the friction between his own company and others, well aware that the white men needed to present a united front to hostile natives.

He slowed down his journey so that the French Canadian traders could catch up and join him. The war bands of Gros Ventres were reported to be along the river, but the information was uncertain. They passed the black timbers of the South Bend Fort which had been attacked and burned to the ground by the Prairie 'Fall' Indians in 1794.

"Bloody Mary" moaned John "I'm being eaten alive by these goddamned mosquitoes!"

"Perhaps we should be thankful that it's been a dry summer and there aren't so many this year" observed Peter dryly.

"I think they are on to the buffalo blood" said a man with them. "We've killed seven".

"Is that mosquitoes or buffalo?" quipped John, slapping wildly at the back of his neck.

"He obviously means mosquitoes! " said another man "Did you notice the grasshoppers? There's millions o' the little divils. We would'a eaten them with the potatoes back in the old country. If we'd had potatoes!"

They laughed.

"Perhaps we could build a fire to drive off the mozzies, Patrick?"

"In the canoe? Don't be stupid Geordie. Even if we built one and towed it, it would catch up wid us, you can bet. Anyway, the miserable little buggers would be warming their sharp noses on it!".

Peter called a halt. "I think it's about time that we took a break lads. Start a fire, Geordie, we'll dry some meat and make a meal at the same time. Take some for the others, too"

They rested from pulling the travois laden with buffalo meat.

Two other men had walked behind and to the sides, carrying several muskets. Both guards stayed alert and faced outwards for protection.

"Gentle Jaisus! " bawled Patrick. "Oi've been stung!" He hopped around on one foot.

On the ground were patches of cactus each covered with long, sharp, needle-like points. A small patch of them had penetrated Patrick's moccasin.

Having helped extract them, Peter warned the rest of the men to be careful and, whenever possible in future, to wear boots.

He wrote a description of the cactus in his journal. It was the second of such plants that he had seen since 1793.

After the fire had been put out, they were met at the landing place, loaded their spoils and set off on the river once again.

Next day, they pulled into the bank to rest, attend to the calls of nature and wash.

A dog raced down the bank, barking.

"Jaisus" breathed Patrick "That means Indians!" and they scrambled back into the canoes and paddled away from the shore. A couple of miles away there was a small island. They circled to the far side and set up camp, nervously watching the mainland.

They smelled campfire smoke which occasionally drifted weakly towards them, but saw no-one. From the first contact on the 6th September, two men kept guard all night, but hardly anyone slept. They hoped that the Northwesters would join them in case the Indians turned out to be unfriendly and they waited on the island until 9th September.

They moved on and Peter left a message for the French informing them that he had held back for 13 days since leaving the mouth of the branch in the hopes of joining forces.

The land became drier and sandier. Many creek beds were empty of water.

"We'll go ashore for fresh water" Peter decided and took two men.

The weather was cool but pleasant. They sloshed ashore at a small inlet where a trickle of water could be seen.

Each man carried two buffalo hide containers. In a gully surrounding the stream, were several large boulders.

They unslung their containers and approached the water.

A form appeared from behind a large rock, stood up to a height of seven feet and growled threateningly.

A grizzly bear, the first they had seen!. They grabbed their containers and fled back to the safety of their boats. The animal must have been in a good mood for it didn't chase them.

From the 14th to 21st, Fidler, lapsing into his Derbyshire dialect, recorded that he had been 'very badly' but was beginning to feel better.

No pursuers, friend or foe, caught up with them as they neared their destination.

They eventually settled near Medicine Hat, in the middle of the prairies, where the landscape undulated in every direction without stick or bush. There were no white men within several hundreds of miles in most directions. To the south and southwest, there were Spaniards and some French traders who had visited the Mandan tribe, but not stayed.

So, on 26th September 1800, Fidler decided to build on the other side of the river.

Before doing so, he called a meeting.

"We've got to where we were going without harm, with the exception of Patrick and his big toe, of course!"

He looked around at the suntanned bearded faces.

"Although I think my hair is a bit whiter after meeting the bear."

Most of the men chuckled and relaxed.

"This is it, then. I intend to build Chesterfield House over there. We shall start the foundations today. Everybody has a job, some of you have two. There are few trees you will notice. In fact, you can hardly miss it! There are some, however, in the small valleys. Cottonwoods. Not perfect, but they'll suffice. Thomas will set up a sawpit and fix handles to the axe heads. With the exception of the rota for guards, we'll all be involved in cutting, trimming, dragging timber. It's important to realise that we shall be visited by some very unstable and potentially hostile locals, so sturdiness of design is most important.

When they get here, be aware of how you behave with them at all times. Most of you know that already, but a couple of you haven't dealt with hostiles before. Learn from the others who have."

He looked around again. They were hanging on to his every word.

"I expect that firearms will become an extension of you. But don't use them except when it is absolutely necessary. Remember, muskets are little use beyond 50 feet. Arrows can travel just as far and often further."

"How big is the House gonna be, Peter?"

"I've been told that we can construct one about 30 feet by 13 feet, including victualling shed and trading room. When we've done that, which should be towards the end of next month, we'll lay out and start to build a dwelling house 51 feet long and 19 feet wide. It will have cellars, chimneys, a wooden floor, adobe walls, parchment windows. Even a flagstaff."

"Bi' Jaisus, I haven't had such luxury since I was in prison!" called out a familiar voice.

Laughter.

"OK lads, let's get to it".

A musket fired.

Everyone turned towards a guard situated at the headland. He was waving his musket horizontally above his head, the signal for unknown people in sight.

Peter strode out to the guard, and stood alongside him. He followed the pointed finger and took a collapsible brass telescope from his pocket.

Two canoes were travelling towards them.

When they came close, the front man called out

"John Wills. X Y Company. Can we come ashore?"

The canoes looked well loaded and Peter welcomed the newcomers.

"We knew you were here. We passed by the Northwesters headed this way about two weeks ago. Three canoes. Pierre Belleau in charge."

Peter stayed where he was as the guard escorted Mr Wells and his men to the camp fire. He needed to think about any significant change in his plans, but there was little to adjust.

When Pierre Belleau arrived, he stepped ashore easily and made straight for Fidler.

Belleau was tall, slim, aristocratic. His hauty air covered a spirit of steel.

"Bon chance, Monsieur Fidler." he greeted with outstretched hand. "It must be five years since we last met"

"Indeed it is, sir" agreed Peter with a smile, replying in French, grasping the firm hand ."I was pleased when told that you would be representing your estimable company."

"You are too kind, Peter. Too kind. But I think it is only fair to tell you that we shall also be building here. Fairly close, too, I understand. That, however, should be to our mutual advantage in the event of hostilities."

"I shall welcome such an arrangement, monsieur. I shall particularly welcome any invitations to dinner that you may have!"

"That you shall, Peter! Now, if you will excuse me, I shall see to my men".

"I shall do the same, sir and I wish you good day".

Shot

He went into the small valley where his men were toiling stripped to the waist in the warm sunshine.

He moved from group to group and exchanged pleasantries with them.

Along two hillocks, two armed guards, screened by bushes, looked outwards across the prairies.

Peter travelled across one hillock and the guard waved.

Peter returned the wave, turned to descend and a tremendous blow struck him in the right thigh, followed by the sound of a gunshot.

He gasped with pain and rolled head over heels down the slope. Several men rushed towards him to offer assistance.

They stripped away the surrounding material, cleaned the wound with fresh water, put on a dressing, and made two splints bound with hide thongs. On a hastily constructed travois, they transported him to camp.

The guard looked in horror from his discharged musket to stricken man and back again. Its trigger had been caught on a protruding twig.

Peter was almost immobile for two weeks, but he took the opportunity to write to Mr Bird and send him a report of progress.

Late in October, he called a meeting with Marcus and John.

"I get the feeling that I'm missing something, lads. It's only 'cause I'm used to being out and about. So I thought to have this meeting and hear first hand news"

"I always think that our meetings are useful, Peter" said John,

his back to a tent screen covering the unfinished doorway.

Mary stood in the background, still, silent and very pregnant.

"I suppose you know that the newcomers under John Wells had established a post at the mouth of the Red Deer River, but so far, no Indians had done business with them.

"Can't say that many have done business with Chesterfield House, either!" said Marcus with a grimace.

"We've excited a bit of curiosity though. Three Gros Ventres, watched us for a couple of days then came to ask for liquor. That small amount you authorised generated a few whoops and yippees. The other three who came at the end of the week were young ones from Buffalo Lake who stayed the night."

John pulled out his pipe and began filling it from a leather bag round his neck.

"Things may be picking up. Three Blackfeet called to ask for tobacco for two Chiefs, one called Bear Coat. Didn't get the other's name. Think it was 'Feathers' or something like that. I noticed there're still about 30 tents of them camped near the Battle River."

"Yep." agreed Marcus, " Three more Fall Indians came this morning, also for tobacco, with three Blackfeet and two Iroquois. There's a 130 tent encampment at Beaver Lake I'm told. They don't look in any hurry to leave. I reckon they'll sleep here."

A knock came on the timber wall.

"Thought ye should know, gentlemen, that 13 tents from that Beaver Lake group have started pitching near the House." said the messenger.

"Thanks Thomas." said John "We should expect them to visit soon".

"Well, as long as they come bearing gifts, I don't mind" said Marcus "But I think we should think about a stockade.

Whatever the temper of the Indians at the moment, it can change. Suddenly. We all know what that means. There's a memorial to it that we passed along the river. I've paced a fence out and I think it would be about 75 feet by 70 feet.. We do need a stockade adjoining the Northwesters building. We could have a common one for both Forts and I thought to have words with the Frenchy about it."

"Mister Ballieu" said Peter mildly. "Yes. I'm sure he'll realise it is in each of our interests to do so. I'll be grateful if you will have a word with him. Let me know the outcome please".

Two weeks later, business had picked up dramatically.

"The Cooper has started to make kegs" said John, at their meeting,drawing deeply on his pipe.

There was a brief silence.

Well, gentlemen" said Peter "We are involved in an experiment. We need pemmican in large quantities. We need to compete with the Northwesters and the New Company. We have to be acceptable to the tribes and have something they want. One thing for certain is that we are be more accessible to them. The prairie tribes had to run the gauntlet of Stones and Crees to get to some of us before. Now they don't. However, I'm always wary about guns. Not only are they liable to turn them on us, but by turning them on other tribes they prevent them from visiting us. We shall always be subject to the ups and downs of the Gros Ventres and Blackfeet!"

He eased himself round in the hard chair and smiled at Mary.

"Mary is expecting our third child, the first week in November, she says, so I need external as well as internal peace for that. I hope to be out and about a little more soon".

They nodded and departed.

He stood, picked up a long walking stick. Mary came forward swiftly and pushed open the canvas screen. He smiled, looked into her black shining eyes and held her hand.

"I think we have been trading well, husband" she said with pride.

Hammering, sawing, somebody singing and another one whistling filled the air. Leaving Mary, he walked slowly around groups of workmen to the trading area.

The storeman hurried out to meet him and placed a chair by the door.

"Nice to see you again, Mr Fidler" he said with pleasure.

"Lot of tribesmen about today going this way and that. "

"What are they up to Joel?".

Joel spat and wiped his mouth with the back of a hand.

"Looks like the Blackfeet are warring with the Snake Indians and the Falls helping them. There must have been 185 tents of 'em out there near the gate"

He squatted in front of Peter.

"'Course, while they warring, they not bringin' us so much meat nor furs!".

"That's right, Joel. Incidentally, what've we done so far?

Joel was pleased at the renewed interest and fetched a hard backed ledger".

"Since we been'd 'ere, we've done pretty well. There's four thousand five hundred and seventy grey foxes, hundred and fifty eight wolves, twenty eight red foxes, twenty six badgers, ten beaver, 3 ordinary cats".

"What about meat, Joel?".

"Let's see. About two thousand pounds of bladder fat and the same and a bit more of dry meat. That's about it I reckons"

He looked searchingly at Peter.

"I hopes ye don't mind me saying so, Mr Fidler, but we's gettin' a mite short of trading goods now. We ain't got but three kettles and practically no cloth fer the tailor. He's moanin' 'cos some of the leadin' lights wants Chiefs' coats and stuff."

"I'm glad you told me that, Joel. Thanks. I'll be sending a couple of men to Edmonton House in a day or so .I'll make sure that gets first priority."

He stood up stiffly.

"As for the trading so far, that's good. Better than I thought. The furs are really a bonus. If the meat comes in at that rate, then our venture has succeeded. Thanks Joel".

Joel beamed with pleasure as Peter walked away.

With two of his own men, bound for Edmonton he met two Blackfeet chiefs near the gate,

He spoke to the chiefs in their own language.

"Greetings brothers. I thank you for offering to take my two men to my own chief at Fort Edmonton. I asked it of you because of your strong spirit which will carry you far, there and back in two moons. They have much to learn from you. I hope that there will be something of interest for you, too, either on the journey or at the Fort."

He turned to the two men.

"You re in good hands, I'm sure you know, lads. Be alert for others, though. George Sutherland is the man you want. He should give you an envelope for me and some trade goods. If he wants to know what the priorities are, tell him 'feathers and fabrics'. My own letter, here, should make it clear".

He shook hands with men and Chiefs alike.

"Good luck".

Spring was on the horizon when the group returned from Edmonton House.

The chief named ' Ac Ko Mok Ki', meaning 'Feathers' met Peter several times and he was able to talk about places he had been and things that he had seen, including routes across the Rockies, the names of hitherto unknown tribes, details of a river called the 'Miss is owri' which travelled long distances into the southern prairies and the Rockies.

He and Peter drew maps which the chief confirmed.

Men were cutting ice, the tailor had one further assistant, helping to produce hats.

The cooper was lost behind a heap of kegs and four men were making soap. Another group was coming to the end of its production of 'carrot tobacco'.

The travellers returned with feathers as requested.

Forty one Ostrich feathers!

"Had a bit 'o trouble last night" said John, "Traded a horse from a large gang of Bloods who came in. They've been at Rocky Mountain House since autumn. They crept round and stole him back. I shall know 'em next time I see 'em though".

"Fetch Marcus in, will you John, I need to talk about our Spring plans" They sat down in the trading room, on seats softened with pelts.

"I heard what you were saying about the horse, John. Sorry I didn't answer straight away. I suppose my mind was full of all sorts of things."

He wriggled to adjust his stiff leg.

"Yes. You're right. Keep and eye open for the culprits. I think we've got other horse stealing problems in the background, as well. The Snakes stole 120 horses from the Muddy River Indians and the latter are off to war with them!

Those Blackfeet who took off a few weeks ago to fight the Snakes have now returned. They didn't find any Snakes and fortunately, they seem to have found nobody! All this potential for warring makes me uneasy and I think we ought to make a few more preparations, just in case. "

"The men have discovered a stand of poplars and I can get them logged and here by the end of the week" said John.

"Unfortunately, those men we sent with the Canadians couldn't find any evergreen trees for pitch and they are back empty handed. They say they went 5 days successive journeying up the river, but came up with nothing."

"I'd like them to try again, in a different direction, with some Blackfoot guides this time. About eighty miles to the southeast of Medicine Hat, there's a hill with Cypress Trees. They should do it." said Peter.

"That will take them all of about ten days, then" said Marcus.

"Incidentally" he went on " I've got men getting ready for the spring move. Some are making up bags of pemmican in 45 pound bags and others making bundles of furs. There are 11 thousand nine hundred and nine to be packed. I estimate that will make nearly 140 bundles."

"Both rivers will be breaking up soon. I want guns and ammunition issued to all the men for when we leave. Also, I think we need more buffalo hides for making ties for the bundles." said Peter. "Will you see to that please, Marcus?".

"X Y Company men set off yesterday." Marcus said standing up. "I've arranged to stow the rest of our things and put them underground before we go as soon as you give the word"

"And the Northwesters are ready to go within the next 24 hours, Marcus" added John "So it looks as though all three houses are going to be abandoned during the summer"

"I reckon that my destination is York Factory via the Rock depot." said Peter thoughtfully. " I have a visit arranged to Cumberland House later in the summer. After that, it's back here for the winter. Assuming of course, that the place is still standing!"

He twisted uncomfortably for a moment to realign his injured leg.

"I shall take some of the summer to complete my mapping. The Company has been approached by Arrowsmith the mappers asking for any information we have. I think we have more than most. I was particularly impressed by the meeting with 'Chief Feathers'. His Indian map gives all kinds of information that we didn't have before. "

His two colleagues nodded with obvious pleasure.

"That would be an achievement, Peter. It makes me think that surveying might be worth while after all!"

It was at Cumberland Fort during the summer that Duncan McGillivray visited.. He was bubbling over with the need to tell about two of David Thompson's men, La Gassi and Le Blanc who had crossed the Rocky Mountains from Rocky Mountain House, the first white men to do it.

Fidler noted down details of the journey with the intention of transferring relevant information to his Great Map, destined for Arrowsmiths.

"I understand that ye'll be returning to the prairies this fall, laddie" said Duncan

Peter nodded without replying.

"Weel, you're likely to be without the pleasure of our company" he said and laughed at his own joke.

Peter laughed too, but with a feeling of apprehension.

"You're telling me that the Fort isn't to be manned ?"

"Aye. That's right laddie. We have other plans afoot." He looked searchingly at Peter."It's nice to know that their details aren't common knowledge yet!"

"Anyway" he went on "Mr Wills and his men should be there"

He turned to depart.

"We leave it to you to decide what you will happen to the fort. You may be able to use the lumber"

He waved and left.

Chesterfield House was as they left it. Everything that had been laid up was safe. Mr Wills duly arrived with the men of XY Company, but no Northwesters appeared.

He had barely settled in when two Blackfoot chiefs came with a letter from Hallett on the North Saskatchewan, advising him that the post at the mouth of Red Deer River was to be abandoned by the Northwesters..

Indians had begun to swarm into the area, and they were surrounded by 3 tribes comprising about 1400 men, women and children.

"I'm not too happy about the Indians using the fort next door. I think we shall have to take it down". He said to Marcus and John who had chosen to accompany him.

"I can get it started today" said John "We'll stack the logs around like barricades until we need them"

John and Marcus left the cabin, only to return minutes later as Peter pored over some maps.

"You ought to come and see this, Peter" said John. Three strangers, Tattoo Indians I'm told, with five women and seven children. I don't think they've seen Europeans before 'cos they certainly gave us some strange looks!"

Peter laid down his tools and went into the autumn sunshine. The Indians were from the eastern edges of the mountains, far to the south and had taken over 6 weeks to get here. He soon discovered that their language was similar to that of the Fall Indians some of whom could be seen outside the gates acting as escorts. They were of a similar size and features to the Falls, but their gestures and manners were different. His conversation elicited the information that they were a tribe of about 100 tents, fairly large by prairie standards.

They had barely left when a Blackfoot chief, called Fatman called.

He was the fattest Indian among the numerous tribes that traded at the

109

settlements and it was estimated that he was about 7 feet around the stomach and equally fat all over!

Their concern about the lack of buffalo came to a rapid end. Millions, stretching to the horizon, surrounded the fort. Peter stowed 198 quarters of buffalo meat to eat for the spring.

Winter set in with a vengeance. Indians, traders, buffalo all suffered. Blizzards raged, freezing all before them. Even the old Indians said they had never known such weather before.

Several Canadians arrived with letters from the Saskatchewan, but with feet and lower limbs so frozen hat they were expected to lose their toes and most of each foot.

Teepees banked with snow became ice towers and their occupants sometimes froze.

Courageous women faced the howling weather to gather frozen sticks for firewood and occasionally never returned. Of those who made it, the fire consumed the sticks faster than they could collect them.

The Gros Ventres believed that they were suffering more than most and that the gods had deserted them since early the previous year.

Even the Blackfeet told of defeats that had accompanied the Gros Ventres when the Southern and Stone Indians had killed 14 men and 60 women and children during the past 8 weeks.

A woman scalped by the Stones was left behind by the Gros Ventres. Her head was like dry bone, exposed to weather for some time.

Then the Blackfeet and Gros Ventres came to blows. The former fell out with Fidler as he attempted to act as peacemaker. They swore never to use the Company again, which would have been a great loss to the House.

In January, 70 young Blackfeet returned from a campaign. On the way back they had met 10 Snake Indians.

The young Blackfoot War Chief rode up to the gates.

"Here are your friends" he sneered and signalled the braves behind him.

Several horses walked by and from each a corpse was tossed. Eight out of the ten Snakes had been smoked out of bear holes where they had taken refuge.

Possessing guns and horses, the Blackfeet were now able to turn the tables on their gun-bearing Cree enemies and the horse-riding Snakes. Their time had come and they cultivated bad relations with Snakes, Sioux, Cree, Crow, Kootenay, Assiniboine, Nez Perce and Gros Ventres. They drove the tribes to the far ends of the area and became masters of the Montana and Canadian Prairies.

The Gros Ventres seethed with hatred and resentment. They had been beaten by Blackfeet, Cree and Stones, suffered from smallpox, cruelly injured by winter.

It came to its climax in February.

Peter visited John Wills at the XY Company House.

"God's truth! " gasped John as the hillocks on the landwards side filled suddenly with about 70 Gros Ventres, who rode backwards and forwards, firing at any head shown.

"Lock the gates, quickly" he shouted, unnecessarily as it happened.

The gates were shut and barred.

"Joe, Pierre, fire in their general direction, but be careful not to kill anybody"

Two Indians stood on horseback and began to scale the fort wall. As the head of the first appeared above the stockade, Fidler knocked him to the ground and Wills dislodged the other. The attackers stood up, dazed and walked away leading their horses.

After an hour, the Indians withdrew. No-one had been seriously injured, but they wanted blood.

"Oh no!" groaned John.

Approaching the Fort were two Canadian free traders and a small band of Iroquois. The latter had left Montreal the previous summer and had been trying their luck to the west.

They passed unscathed through the band of Gros Ventres and slipped through the small gate into the Fort.

John and Peter descended to meet the travellers.

"We don't intend to stay long" said one of the Canadians. "We shall leave tomorrow early and make friends with the Gros Ventres."

"An unlikely proposition at the moment " said John. "You are welcome to stay as long as you like, certainly until matters cool down"

Next day, the visitors split into two groups and left. One group joined a camp of Blackfeet and the other including the 2 Iroquois went to join the Gros Ventres who greeted them cordially and accepted their peace offerings.

Later, about 4 miles from the Fort, they attacked the Iroquois, mutilated and scalped them.

The Canadians escaped back to the Fort and told the story.

111

Next day, Fidler went to meet Gros Ventres traders at the House gates.

"We are unhappy with your killing of the 2 Iroquois" he told them "It was unnecessary and is bad for our business and therefore yours."

The two chiefs and their band made no movement or gesture. Stoney-faced they remained silent.

"I have two more distant Indian visitors coming to see me within a few days. I trust that you will not attack them. In the meantime, until they arrive safely, I will not trade with you".

They looked at him for long moments. One chief swung around and grunted. The band turned its back on Peter and walked through the gates to their horses.

Marcus came to see him that afternoon.

"A couple of Blackfeet called by earlier. Those Gros Ventres who came have dug up the bodies of the 2 Iroquois and cut off their hands and feet. They've taken them back home to their tents, which are only about three-quarters of a mile away."

"There isn't anything to be done at this stage, Marcus. Just leave the matter and hope that it means that our live Iroquois will be safe!"

It was too much to hope for.

Blackfeet were camped around the fort, when Gros Ventres attacked out of nowhere. A desperate battle ensued, brushing up against the stockade.

The men inside manned the walls but did not fire as the Indians fought hand to hand.

Then, the will departed and Gros Ventres withdrew. Miraculously, no-one was killed, but the Blackfeet removed their wounded.

The following day, over 200 Gros Ventres braves rode past the gates in a challenging manner.

They rode off down the river and came back in the afternoon on the opposite side of the river.

They were sporting scalps on the ends of long poles, belonging to 10 Iroquois and 2 Canadians. They shouted that they would do the same to those in the fort.

"The Canadian master is here, with his men and women" said Marcus.

"I'll come out to meet him" said Fidler.

"Welcome, John" he greeted John Wills "I have room for you if you wish to stay".

"Thanks Peter. I thought you would help. Circumstances are rather bleak at the moment and I daren't risk the lives of my people. We'll pitch in and help in order to pay our way"

"Consider yourselves our guests, John. What do you intend to do about your House?"

"I'd like your help to burn it and cut down the stockade. I don't want the Fall Indians using it, especially as a harbour. "

"Yep. See what you mean. We need to go past it to fetch water. I'll arrange it. We have 19 men besides a visitor from the Northwesters. How many are you?"

"We are 16 men now, Peter, plus the two who lost their feet last winter"

"So, that makes us 37. I think they will be unlikely to attack us in the fort now".

The Cooper came down from the lookout above the gate.

"You'll not believe this, Mr Fidler, but there's some o'them savages a'knockin' at the gate, askin' to trade!"

"Excuse me will you John, while I go and take a look?".

Peter climbed the ladders and stood in full view of the truculent Indians.

"What is it you want from us? Have you brought back to life the Iroquois that you killed ? Or the Canadians?."

The Indians made no reply. Their horses jittered in small movements below.

Peter heard the cocking of firearms beside him. He turned to find several XY men about to shoot into the crowd below.

"No! " he cried and knocked up the muskets.

"Leave this to me!"

He turned back to the restless group.

"I know the chiefs who are responsible for killing our friends. You know them too. I will not trade until those chiefs come to me and talk".

John Wills was beside him.

"Good idea" he said "I reckon we should get the chiefs in, kill 'em and hang the principal chief over the stockade. Then kill about 30 others that we let in. Not one of the buggers to get out again! That would show 'em that we mean business and aren't to be trifled with!"

The horsemen swirled around, then broke and trotted away without comment.

They returned next day.

Peter ascended the ladder to the position above the gates.

"What do you want this time?" he asked."We do not intend to trade with you".

A chief moved forward.

"Lean Bear and I, Buffalo Coat will enter with braves" he said.

There was a hum of anger among the fort's men.

"We shall leave our weapons behind" said Lean Bear.

Peter thought.

"Open the smaller gate and let them in one at a time. Keep 'em covered. Judging by the movement, I think there'll be a couple of dozen. Don't let 'em wander off anywhere."

Then in a louder voice in the Indian language. "Shoot anyone who enters too far!".

The chiefs dismounted and entered in single file followed by 30 braves.

Peter descended from the platform and stood in front of the chiefs.

He folded his arms, but said nothing, looked squarely into their eyes in turn, then concentrated on Lean Bear.

"I hear that you have spoken our names" said Lean Bear.

Peter said nothing.

"We cannot bear the blame of guilt for what our young men have done!."

Peter still said nothing.

"The distant foreigners should not come to our land to hunt. They have their own lands beyond the great waters. They have no blood with our tribes. However, we shall let you bury them and the Canadians tomorrow. We shall give you safe conduct from the Blackfeet who are the cause of all our ills."

Peter continued to listen.

There seemed to be an edge of desperation in the chief's voice.

"My people's hearts are low at the troubles we have suffered. The young men will not listen to us, neither will they hunt or trap. While they are warring, they are not doing either."

He stopped speaking and Buffalo Coat edged forwards.

"Because of the circumstances, we have nothing to trade with you at this time. No furs. No meat. But things are changing for the better. We shall be able to go out and hunt during the summer. We shall hunt and trap well. Enough for you to give us credit now "

Peter thought, then made his reply.

"I am truly sorry that things have been as they have, both for you, for us and for our other friends. I need to think about your offer. If you will come tomorrow, then I shall give you my answer"

There was silence, then movement as the chiefs went past him through the gate.

They didn't return.

A Blackfoot trader visiting the trading room, laughed when he was told the story.

" The Gros Ventres will have little chance to hunt, soon. The Assiniboines and Crees even now are planning to attack them in a few weeks time!".

Once again the Gros Ventres tribe broke its promise.

That afternoon, they moved away and headed for the Missouri River. They tried to form an alliance with the Tattoos and Crows to invade the Canadian Prairies and then annihilate the causes of their troubles, the Crees, Assiniboines, Blackfeet and all traders.

It was the last that was seen of them in the north.

A little later, in April, Fidler and his men left the area for good. Neither Hudson's Bay nor the XY House were available to trade at that location.

CHAPTER 8

Violence Unleashed

(1802 - 1806)

London England.

"I feel that we should be reestablishing our trade at Chipewyan on both Lake Athabasca and Peace River" said the stout member with the large cigar.

"Robert is right!" said his neighbour, a thin-faced soberly dressed churchman. We have lost several years of trade from the Chipewyan Indians!"

"That's because the North West Company is on the spot and we are not!" interjected a third member, sipping at a glass of claret.

"Didn't realise you were one of these poet chappies, Roger!"

Roger frowned, missing the point.

"'On the spot'. 'we are not'. Rhymes, don't you see?"

Roger's frown disappeared.

"Dashed clever of me, what?".

Robert carried on doggedly.

"It will be a most difficult and dangerous project. Even discouraging. We shall need a good man to accomplish it."

"I believe we already have the man" said a tall figure lounging at the back of the room.

"And who do you have in mind, Cavendish?".

Cavendish turned towards the group around the table. "At this moment, the map of the Northwest is being compiled by the cartographer, Arrowsmith. Its information has been provided by one of our employees. I have spoken with Dalrymple at the Admiralty. Both he and Captain Cook are impressed by the quality of the cartography. The area concerned is the very one about which we are speaking. The individual concerned speaks several Indian languages, has been with the Company for 14 years and is recognised as a great explorer and trader."

116

He stopped and looked round. He could see that some members knew who he was talking about, others were interested, but he waited for a question.

"Dash my braces, Cavendish! Don't be so deuced secretive! Who the devil is this chap, hey?"

"I think he is alluding to Fidler, Roger"

"Well why didn't he say so!" Roger subsided, muttering.

Robert turned to Cavendish. "He's still a youngster, Cavendish. And there is Turnor"

"With respect Sir Robert, Turnor may be too old for this enterprise. Fidler, I believe, is only thirty-three. He is married to a Cree and is known to the Chipewyans. He is also known to both the North West Company and the XY Company. I'm sure that he's astute enough to cope with both of them, even if they form one company, as they are talking of doing".

"We can't provide him with much money" said the Churchman. "Certainly not enough to compete with the resources available to the two Montreal Companies. We have had a poor return on our investments this year, already! And the war is making us poorer.!"

Several heads nodded in assent.

The Churchman continued.

"If Fidler can't cope with the North Westers and the XY Company, then we shall have much to lose. He may have to fight harder to get his way. He may be an intrepid explorer and fur trader but I've heard that he's soft!" He looked round, triumphantly.

"Perhaps he should continue to heed the teachings of the Church" said Cavendish evenly. "For if any serious consequences should arise from our quarrels it would be very difficult to find redress here, or even on application to the Government"

"Fidler is then nominated. I don't want to repeat all that fol-de-rol. Just a show of hands, gentlemen, 'to direct Fidler to set up posts at Chipewyan'."

It was unanimous.

"Let it be made known, then" said the Chairman, banging his gavel.

Builds Mansfield & Nottingham Houses

Thomas Swain read the letter.

"So they are expecting you to take-on the big boys with 17 men!".

117

"Seems so!" said Fidler quietly. "Good job that we've always maintained reasonable relations with representatives of the Northwesters and the XY Company."

But Peter knew that this was to be the most challenging of his assignments. "We shall be taking five canoes, Thomas, and sixteen men to build two trading houses. One will be at the Athapascow Lake and the other up Peace River."

Thomas Swain was excited at the prospect.

"Mr Tomison had some difficulty recruiting men to go to that country" he said. "The men think that there is only fish to live on, it's a very long way, and there's a lot of carrying to be done!"

"There's some truth in all that, Thomas. However, one of the reasons for establishing the Peace River post is to collect pemmican for our men. I'll make that clear to them before we go".

It wasn't very long before Fidler's party realised that t the competitors were up to something.

Indians along the way avoided them. It was the third day, when Fidler met some relations of his wife, that he was told about the behaviour of the Northwester men.

"They are ahead of you by half a day" said Lean Hound. " They have beaten a number of our people as an example to the rest. They are told not to help you at all"

The Crees left a portion of moose for Fidler and slipped silently into the undergrowth.

Peter was concerned about the welfare of his accompanying wife and three children, but she reassured him that she and they were well and the next day, Mary tracked a moose which the men killed.

"We got company!" growled Thomas, with a jerk of his head.

Peter identified Mr Leith of the XY Company, with 5 canoes.

"How are ye Fidler" he bellowed. "We'd be happy to escort you part of the way. We're off to the Peace River Country"

"Pleased to see you sir" said Peter "Feel free to join us"

"We passed James MacKenzie a wee ways back. He's off to the Athabasca and Slave Lakes with 5 canoes"

"Tomorrow, Mr Swain will be leaving us. He is taking three canoes and nine men to a similar destination as yourself, the Peace River. He will be establishing a trading post there. I think he will call it Mansfield House.

That will be about 200 miles west as the crow flies, from Chipewyan. He will be pleased to accompany you."

Swain and Leith split off the next day and went their own way.

Fidler continued with the remaining eight men, looking for a site until, eventually, he was within three-quarters of a mile of the Northwester's post.

There, he built Nottingham House.

All three companies now had houses in the vicinity of Fort Chipewyan.

During the first evening, several Indians came cautiously into the construction area.

Peter recognised two of them and strode out to greet them.

"We would like to resume trading with you but we are fearful of the Northwesters" one explained.

Mr Leith and his 15 men didn't fare very well at their post on the Peace River.

Northwesters circulated among the resident Beaver Indians and spread malicious gossip along with threats and violence.

The Beavers blamed all misfortune on the XY Company and drove them away. It was the third time that XY had tried and failed.

Swain and his small band of men at Mansfield House did a little better than Leith. But not for long.

The Beavers were not biased against Hudson's Bay and several old men remembered the days when they had been treated decently and fairly by them.

But now, the Northwesters poured liquor into the Beavers and by brutality and trickery, drove them away.

Fidler recorded during October that similar practices were being perpetrated at Nottingham House.

"One of our friends, a Chief, was pillaged of 10 beaver skin and one good wolf as he passed the Old Company (Northwester's) House."

Swain acquired very few furs, but worse than that, no pemmican.

In January, he reported with his men to Nottingham House, reporting that it was no use trying to do business up the Peace River. It was a dilemma. It was necessary to acquire pemmican from Peace River for Nottingham House for their trip out in the Spring.

Fidler encouraged his men to catch more fish to use in the Spring.

In the meantime, he felt it necessary to plan ahead for next year and he wrote to Tomison outlining a strategy.

He proposed that provisions should be available at Cumberland House ready for an early journey next Summer, then they could be on site and operating before the North Westers arrived.

Swain was sent to contact Indians who were in debt to the Company. He travelled with an XY Company group with whom they had good relations.

They found that the Indians had already been visited by Northwesters and threatened with beatings and worse if they continued to trade with Swain.

The Indians genuinely wanted to trade, to pay their debts, but on numerous occasions, they were accosted, robbed and beaten by Northwester employees.

At Nottingham House, Fidler was having trouble with a group of Northwesters who set up a tent near the entrance to the House and frightened away Indian traders. It was coming to the end of the trading season and many of them had furs to trade.

Fidler decided to call at the Northwesters fort, but when he arrived there, they refused him entry and turned him away.

Peter's first daughter, Sally was born on November 26th 1802 in Fort Chipewyan, at 5 minutes after 2 in the morning.

Winter passed and Spring arrived.

"James " he said to James Kirkness, "I shall be taking 9 men with me in May. The exact date hasn't been decided yet, but I want to leave you in charge for the summer. It should be easier than the winter we have just gone through. I hope to report to Cumberland House and then return for the next season".

"What do you want me to do, Peter?" asked Thomas Swain.

"I think that another try at Mansfield House could be successful now. Anyway, I'd like you to go there and see what you can do, Thomas."

"How many men can be spared to accompany me?"

"I think that 4 will probably suffice, Thomas. There maybe a chance of getting a new toehold at Mansfield during the summer when the opposition is away".

"I think you ought to know that there is considerable unrest among the men, Peter. They have had a bellyful this winter and several of them are not prepared to come back."

John Kirklees stroked his long beard.

"I think that a few of them are holding out for more money, Thomas. If the Company will pay them more, I think they'll stick".

"That may well be true, John" said Thomas, nodding. "But there are the other reasons. For example, a couple of them watched James MacKenzie beat up on that Indian boy at our gate who came to pay the credit he owed. If their Master is like that, what can we expect from his men? Given a few more minutes and Campbell would have shot him!"

"Yep. That's true. Thought about it myself. Even more so when they burned our canoe!. Only the realisation that we are seriously outnumbered stops me from shooting the hell out of them sometimes".

"It's understandable, John" said Peter quietly "But remember, we don't have to live here during the summer. The Indians do. And we wouldn't be able to protect them. Nor do we want an uprising. So playing it cool is the proper thing to do at this stage. Agreeed?"

The two men nodded.

The Northwesters continued to bribe the Indians with rum but the resultant drop in trapping showed that there would be insufficient to repay that outlay.

John rushed in to the main house.

"The goddamn 'Westers are up to something! They've carried timber up near our main gate!"

Peter closed his ledger and went to see for himself.

He mounted the gate ladder and stood on the ledge. He counted twenty men scurrying around, pulling logs and piling them nearby.

Several men with axes and other tools were beginning to shape the timber.

John mounted the steps and stood alongside Peter.

"Goddam sonsabitches are building a watch-house near our gate. Say it's to watch who comes in and outta our place! Can you believe it! No Indians will dare come here now!"

"I guess that's part of the idea" said Peter thoughtfully. There was resignation in his voice.

"We can always burn the goddam thing down when they've done" growled John.

"We could, but we shan't" said Peter. "It looks far enough away to be considered a legal and independent unit even though we might not think so".

He turned with a sigh while John continued to glower at the workmen.

"I don't know whether it will turn the tables, or what it will achieve exactly, but I'd like to use the same tactics" he confided to John at supper.

"Can you fix it for a tent with two men to take up a position where they can see into the Westers camp? Tonight?".

"Sure can" said John enthusiastically. "In fact, I'll start it off myself. That should give the sonsabitches something to think about!"

"There's only one problem, John We don't have a tent!"

"No problem, Peter. I think XY will lend us one. I'll go over there tonight then and if we get one, we'll stick it up tomorrow night. OK?"

Peter nodded. He looked thin and tired.

"I've had a report from XY that their up-river crew has returned empty handed. Mainly, I'm told, because the locals are too spoiled by Westers rum. No trapping. Anyway, let's leave the tent up, assuming we get one, for a few weeks and see what happens".

"Quick boss!" A head appeared around the doorway. They's gonna kill each other, on the lake!"

"What the hell's this about" said John and he bustled with Peter into the compound.

A small dark man in knitted woolly had pointed towards the lake. Several dozen yards out, two canoes faced each other. A man stood in each one, balancing precariously. The way their arms were extended indicated that they were brandishing pistols.

Peter shaded his eyes.

"Can't quite make 'em out, can you John"

"Yeah. Its MacKenzie and Leith. Looks serious to me!"

A canoe had been run up on the beach nearby, so John, James and Peter commandeered it. They paddled out to the other company's canoes. Raised, angry voices reached them as they approached. The lake was calm with barely a ripple, but the canoes swayed ominously.

A small gout of water leapt into the air alongside Fidler's canoe, followed instantly by a loud bang.

Another bang followed, leaving no visual trace.

"Stupid bastards are shooting at one another" panted James.

"Lousy shots. I feel safe already" said John.

"Try and keep, me upright, lads. That water looks mighty cold" and Peter put down his paddle and stood up, swaying slightly.

They were within five yards of the antagonists and had just been noticed.

122

"Whattya want, Fidler" snarled MacKenzie, pointing the single-shot pistol at him. Smoke still curled out of its barrel.

"Why, nothing really" replied Fidler calmly. "Heard you boys were having a meeting on the lake and thought to join you. Sociable, like. " He looked around innocently.

"New way of catching fish, though. Shooting 'em!"

The two assailants stared at him in astonishment.

Leith began to laugh and was joined by MacKenzie. Their canoes rocked seriously and they both sat down with a thump.

"God!. You gotta nerve, Fidler. Gotta give you that. A few minutes ago I woulda shot you." said MacKenzie, wiping his eyes.

He turned to Leith.

"You know my feelings. Take notice of 'em. It'll be safer". He gestured with his pistol and the two paddlers took him away.

"I seem to have interrupted a conversation" said Peter, sitting down carefully in the bottom of his canoe.

"You avoided a killing, Peter. Don't know whose, but we'd managed the first round and were ready for the second"

Peter looked at the retiring Westers' canoe.

"We expect to be doing a lot of fishing this winter. If we can help you with any, I shall be pleased to do so."

"We could do with some now" confessed Leith.

"OK. No problem. I'll send round a couple of dozen. Is that all right?"

"That'll be great" said Leith thankfully. "We'd better make for home now" and with a wave, he picked up a paddle and they made off.

"Ugh! Fish" said James.

The winter passed into early spring. Swain had set up a new trading house called Chiswick House on Great Slave Lake.

During the same period, a well-known North Wester, Saint Germain, 'Buffalo Head' died at the age of sixty six. He left behind a family bearing his name. Also, Buffalo Head Hills and Buffalo Head Prairie.

Fidler sat outside on a log, in the weak sunshine, with several men.

"We've made most of the preparations to leave and there isn't too much left to do" he said.

"Some of the Westers from Smoky River have pulled in to their fort yesterday" remarked George.

"Anybody we might know?" said John, blowing into his hot, tin mug.

"Yeah. Davy Thompson. He'll be staying a few days, I'm told"

"David Thompson? " exclaimed John "He's an old buddy of yours, Peter".

"Yes" said Peter.

"Will you be visiting before we leave, Peter?"

"Don't think so" said Peter, curtly "Still some bits for me to do".

"Pity about John Ross." said James, changing the subject. "Gone over to the enemy"

"Which one was he?" asked George.

"I think he was an Aberdonian, but I'm not sure. Surly guy. Stocky. Good worker though. Told he was dosed up with rum on New Years Eve and signed up before he knew it!"

"Never take a free drink from a Wester, is my motto" growled John.

"I dunno. There are some exceptions. Remember old Buffalo Head? Had a clutch of kids. Good guy. Well named, too. Big head with a mass of hair." reminisced James.

"Oh yeah. Remember him. Saint Germain. Told he died this winter. Be about sixty five or six. First guy to report the Buffalo Hills I'm told".

"There'll be a heap of St Germains around the west now that he's gone"

"Hey! Meant to tell you guys. Saw three horses yesterday! Westers brought 'em down river. Must be the first in this region. Looked mighty good, I can tell you!"

"Hate to be a horse that comes from the lush grass country on the Peace River. This area is miserable in comparison" said Peter. He tipped his cup against the building, but nothing came out.

"Well, we'll be gone in a couple of days. Back to civilisation at Cumberland House. New faces, friends. But, all in all, despite the odds, we are still here.

Seventeen men against a hundred and ninety five Westers. They've taken out a hundred and eighty five packs of furs weighing about eighty five pounds each. Most of their stuff was killed by 110 Iroquois out to the Rocky Mountains. So their local expense, high as it is, hasn't done them much good." He said.

James spat into the dust. "I recall how they took over 600 packs from this area in 1800. Only had 126 men. Traded with 246 pieces of goods. One helluva difference now.

Even the XY's have 83 men. At most we have 18."

"If we'd had more men, more trade goods, we could have beat the hell outta the goddam Westers" said Robbie.

"Well, I shan't be sad to leave here" said John. "Two lousy winters on a lousy shore by a lousy lake with lousy neighbours! Who could ask for more?"

"I used to think that Chesterfield House was in a bleak area" commented Peter. "Flat plains every which way. No trees. But this place takes some beating for bleakness."

"Yeah. I agree. But one saving grace at Chesterfield was the buffalo. Millions of 'em. Cooking fires dripping fat!" intoned James hungrily.

"Don't tell me you don't like whitefish, Jim? Lovely grub. Mushy with lotsa green things. Just try and imagine that it's rich, thick, prime, buffalo tongue" said George.

James threw his empty mug at him.

"Roll on Cumberland and the summer".

Summer at Cumberland House came and went.

Peter's report was ignored. He was sent back to Nottingham House in August 1804 with Thomas Swain two canoes and eight men.

Anticipating the worst, he made arrangements to determine whether trading should be continued or not.

On the third day, they were signalled by three indians, two Crees and an Iroquois.

Peter's canoe pulled towards them and they lay alongside.

After the traditional friendship greetings, one of the Crees said

"There has been trouble at Chipewyan"

"Trouble? What kind of trouble my friend?"

"The people have been unable to stomach the constant insults and bullying of the white men at Chipewyan. So, my people killed two of their chiefs at Font du Lac were and burned their fort. They then killed four more of their tribe at Chipewyan".

After they had parted, Fidler entered in his diary "If it is indeed true, then it is richly deserved by the Canadians who are very severe with them"

Further along the river they were hailed from the shore by a small group of Cree Indians.

"Pull over" instructed Peter. "I know some of them"

He stepped ashore and was met by their leader who was obviously pleased to see him.

125

"What are you doing so far from home?" asked Peter, passing along the pipe.

"I have unfortunate news for you, brother" said the man."We were involved in the death of four Canadians from Chipewyan and we live in fear of revenge. Now that you will be there, we shall move closer to our home"

Peter left them, and his small party arrived at Nottingham House on September 11th and sent Swain and four men to Great Slave Lake.

On 12th October, Mary bore him, another child and at this time, Fidler changed the name of Nottingham House to Fort Chipewyan and headed his records accordingly.

The winter dragged on remorselessly, similar to the preceding year. Indians were afraid to trade, food was scarce. On 13th January, as agreed, he sent two men on the 370 mile journey through ice and snow to Isle-A-La-Crosse to report and establish whether he was to keep Nottingham for 1805 - 1806 season. They accomplished the outward journey in 17 days.

After resting for two weeks, they returned, taking 16 days. Their message was to continue trading next year.

Fidler maintained good relations with the XY Company

On 6th May, a messenger arrived at the Northwesters fort to inform them that they and the XY Company had amalgamated.

It had been thought that such a move was afoot, and was confirmed when the Mater sent a message to Peter.

It was short and not too sweet.

"We are gonna drive Hudson's Bay from the Athabasca region"
it said..

Peter realised that the task would be even more difficult than it had been before.

The new Head of the joint company was William MacGillivray, friend of Alexander MacKenzie of the XY company, both of whom Peter had met before.

Celebrations took place at both company posts. Flags were hoisted and shots fired.

A man entered the stock room, carrying a note .

"From the Westers, Mr Fidler" he said.

It was a letter from James MacKenzie inviting Fidler and his men 'to tea'.

126

"What's the purpose of that?" queried George, tying bundles of furs.

"I've a sneaking feeling it's to let us know that all is now hopeless, George. But I think we'll go and play it by ear. Let the men know"

Food was plentiful, and liquor was available. Fidler's men ate well but drank little.

"I suppose ye'll be packing up now, Fidler?" said a man named McCloud.

"Yes, we will at the end of the season" said Peter politely.

McCloud's eyes were red and his face flushed.

"Ye've no right being in this quarter, Fidler. We'll drive ye out of it if ye don't decide to pull out on your own!. Ye'll walk over our bodies before we let a single Indian into your House!"

Peter and his men held their tempers and left the fort.

That night, the timber which had been stacked near the river with great effort, was fired.

Swain came down from Slave Lake to find out what was planned for summer.

Fidler sent three men to Chiswick House and instructed Thomas to remain at Nottingham for the summer.

Black Terror

It was their first meeting with the giant, Samuel Black a Highlander who had arrived in 1802 to work for his uncle's employer, the North West Company. At the merger with XY Company, he was sent to Chipewyan.

He barged into Nottingham at the beginning of departure preparations and insisted on seeing everything.

With which introduction Peter departed.

The next season, 1805-1806, Peter returned to Nottingham House."We've got the same problem as last year, Peter" said Thomas. " a Northwester whas been sent ahead from Isle-A-La-Crosse to drive away all game and instruct Indians not to deal with Fidler. The Goddamm Westers have sprung up like mushrooms! Every time we pass a post, one or more of their men is sent out ahead of us!"

Worse was to follow.

Hungry and tired, they arrived at Nottingham House on September 11th.

"Do you see what I see" gaped Tomas in disbelief.

The Westers had erected a building a mere 200 yards away and a tent within four yards of Hudson's Bay's House.

As they unpacked, Peter gave his instructions.

" Food stocks are already low, lads so I'll send men out to trap ducks which were massing for migration."

Samuel Black, with several men, followed them and scared away the birds.

The same day, Black and his gang pulled up the Hudson's Bay garden and tried to set fire to the House.

Black was aware that Fidler had been instructed not to fight back which increased his bullying. He had been given the task of wearing Fidler and his men down so that they would surrender and leave the region.

Fidler's men were completely cowed by this huge, vicious man who swaggered around. They swore that they would never return to Nottingham House again.

"I don't know what we can do, Peter" said Thomas one morning. "Things aren't getting any better here. We'll have to do something. Our men will crack and take off if we don't. It's not that we couldn't manage him on his own, but he's got his gang around him all the time. Two or three of our men have sworn to kill him but I've restrained them".

"I've given it a lot of thought, Thomas. Short of killing him, there isn't much else to do. However, I do have one idea that may work. They are doing what they are doing because of our threat to their trade. If I promise not to trade until we've leave, they may relent. Call him off. What do you think?"

"It will seem a bit pointless being here if we do that. But I can't think of much else". Thomas said, frowning.

"I think we'll take a stroll over to the Westers' fort. " said Peter.

MacKenzie was delighted with Peter's suggestion.

"What you're saying, man, is that ye'll cease trading now until next season, hey?. Well, that's not good enough."

He lit a cheroot and blew smoke into the air.

"I want a clear run for the next two seasons. None of your company here for the next two years. That's the deal, then I'll call Black off. Agreed?"

"That's agreed, provided you supply us with supplies. Meat, mainly".

MacKenzie glowed. "Meat. Weel, that's no a problem for us, Fidler. I'll let ye have ten moose for the winter. "

"Also, I feel that we would acquire up to a hundred beaver if we continued trading."

"All right" said MacKenzie testily."A hundred prime, made, beaver. I'll even throw in a supply of pemmican to support you on the way out. Satisfied?"

"I'm very grateful, MacKenzie. You drive a hard bargain" said Peter. He held out his hand.

MacKenzie looked at it as though it was a poisonous snake.

"McCloud will see you out" he snapped and turned his back.

"What the hell are we going to do for the rest of the season" asked Swain as they trudged back to the House.

"Take up fishing, I guess" said Peter.

But Black wasn't restrained. He came with four men and dismantled the watch house. He then re-erected it within ten yards of Hudson's Bay door.

MacKenzie was angrily unsympathetic.

"I'll get him to take it down and build it in front of your window next time" he shouted.

Black's next move was to tear off a strip of the bark roof and mount it on top of their chimney. The smoke drove them outside and a fire started in the chimney, very near to setting the building alight. It was a good job they were at home otherwise it may have burned the house down.

At the end of December, Fidler sent two men to Isle A La Crosse with a message notifying headquarters of his situation and pointed out that it would be useless to return next year.

Bully Black was now in full swing.

When the messengers returned in February, he forced his way into Nottingham House

"I wanna see all you've got" he bawled. "All the stuff you've brought back".

He grabbed the rolls brought by the two messengers and tipped them upside down on the floor.

"Not very goddamn tidy are we!" he snarled.

He turned as Peter came into the room.

"What is it that you want, Mr Black?"

"Nothing you got! It's what they've got. "He pointed a huge finger at the two men in turn and they shrank back.

"It would probably be better for all of us if you behaved like a civilised man, Mr Black", said Peter quietly.

129

Black turned, took one pace forwards and towered over Fidler.

"Listen, you sonnofabitch, I don't care about you nor MacKenzie nor the other goddamn Company. When I says jump, you're gonna jump, savvy?"

He glared at Fidler who stood straight and pale but unflinching.

"You really are something of an arsehole Mr Black, but go ahead and make an idiot of yourself. Look in their things if you will. There's nothing that I wouldn't want you to see".

He turned and walked to the doorway.

"And when you've seen your fill, then leave this post".

That night, the whole building was shaken by howling and banging.

Peter went to investigate, but the rowdies ran away, laughing and shouting.

Next day, Peter sent a message to MacKenzie asking him to stop his men from howling during the night and beating on the walls.

During the next and subsequent nights, the noise and beating continued for hours on end. Billets of timber and axe handles were used to bang the building until plaster fell out..

MacKenzie promised to try restrain Black.

"Black wants to see you Mr Fidler. He's banging at the door. I don't think we can hold him fer long"

"All right, John Let him in. Let's see what he wants."

Black swaggered into the trading room and leaned against the wall with one leg crossed and picked his teeth with a heavy knife. Indoors, his huge frame was even more ominous than outdoors.

"What the hell's this I hear about you fantasizing to MacKenzie" he snarled. "We never touched you and if we did, you'd soon know it!"

Peter sat at a small table near the window. His records and other documents were open in front of him.

"What exactly do you want, Mr Black?"

"Well, I'll tell you what I want. I want you to pick up that pen and write to MacKenzie telling him how you had a bad night and imagined folks outside a'banging and a'singing. That's what I want!"

"Are you a reader, Mr Black?"

Black gave a grunt of disgust.

"Huh. Me ?A reader. Not on your life. Don't need none of that sissy English stuff. No sir. These are good enough for me" He showed a huge clenched fist.

"Now git that goddamned note writ".

Peter picked up quill and paper. He wrote a brief note to MacKenzie asking him to restrain Black.

On completion, he sealed it with sealing wax and passed it to Black who looked suspiciously at the red wax.

"That's how he'll know it's from me" Peter said calmly.

MacKenzie wrote back indicating that he would have words with Black. That same night, someone fired several shots outside Peter's window and voices set up another night of unearthly howling.

When the ice had cleared, Fidler and Swain went over to the Northwesters' Fort to collect the promised furs and food.

MacKenzie refused to honour his agreement.

Peter wrote a finale in his diary.

"We all left this quarter".

William Auld of Churchill House was very sarcastic about Fidler, commenting about Fidler's "mean and spaniel-like behaviour".

But Peter worked directly under York House where perceptions were different.

Two years later, Auld spent a winter at Reindeer Lake with Fidler, where the activities of the Northwesters continued.

His opinions changed.

CHAPTER 9

More Violence & Rape

(1806 - 1811)

Mary walked into the small room which Peter used as his office and library in Cumberland House.

She carried a mug of Indian tea. Peter's head was lowered over a ledger and as he studied, he rubbed his right ear absent-mindedly with a goose quill.

He didn't stir when she entered. Her movements were silent, footsteps shielded by soft moccasins.

He looked up, slightly startled, as her shadow fell across the table top. Then he smiled, took the mug, but held on to her arm.

"How are you finding things here, Mary?" he asked "A big improvement on Nottingham House!"

She smiled.

"Well, plenty fish, many buffalo. Sometimes, moose meat. Our people not afraid to trade with us. Much better than Nottingham House and its bad spirits. Enemy not so bad here. Children happy."

"You're right, Mary. We have all those things and more. The children seem more settled and that's understandable. We even get on with the Northwesters next door! I don't know how long this life is going to last, but we'll make the most of it".

Mary sat on an upturned rum keg, one of several used as chairs. She reached forward, took his mug and sipped at it.

"Nor'westers not so strong here. Not too many people. We got plenty enough people if they make trouble. I think they not want trouble."

"That's true, too, love. I'm glad they don't use the same tactics that were used at Chipewyan. I don't think we could have stood a lot more of that!"

Mary looked searchingly at Fidler as she passed back the mug. Her man was thirty-seven years of age. He had been in the Company's service for eighteen years. The stresses of Lake Athabasca had taken their toll.

"I have put out a change of clothes for you"

"Change of clothes? What for, love?"

132

"You forget everything! Tonight, we go to dinner with Northwesters !"

"My God!. So we do!. It had completely slipped my mind. I sometimes wonder what I would do without you to keep me organised"

He leaned forward and looped an arm around her neck, stretched forward to kiss her on full lips, lingeringly. She responded then pushed him away.

"Not time" she said, her eyes sparkling and face flushed. "Finish what you do. I heat water."

She stood up and looked over his shoulder

"What you do?"

"I'm writing to William Auld. He's taken over the reins from Mr Tomison and is in charge at Churchill. He'll be my boss now although I have heard that Tomison went home to England, couldn't settle and has got another job with the Company."

She sat down again.

"I hear that Tomison want to go to Lake Athabaska by another trail. He already had meeting with Auld. You best man for Lake Athabaska journey. I think they ask you to go, too"

He looked at her serious face. Her lips were slightly open, the tip of a pink tongue sat in one corner of her startlingly white teeth.

Much of her speculation came from knowledgeable sources; friends, relatives, travellers, who depended on their observations to gather information

He heaved a huge sigh, stood and stretched upwards.

His barrel-seat rocked unsteadily.

"I hadn't thought that far ahead, love but it seems sensible".

She too stood and they were inches from each other.

He placed both hands at her waist and marvelled that she had kept such a good figure after childbirth. Her hair was black and glossy, framing dark eyes which could flash or turn to liquid.

He gave another sigh and wrapped both arms around her, holding her tightly against him.

"As long as I have you" he murmured into her right ear, "The rest is worth it and life is good". He nibbled the lobe. She melted and moved against him then, once more, pushed him away playfully.

"You soon be too late for good wash and change!. Finish book and come into house".

She turned and slid noiselessly through the adjoining door.

The time had come for him to leave

Peter stood in the doorway of the cabin

"Well, love, they look ready to go. I don't think we've forgotten anything."

They held hands and looked towards the canoe.

"This is one of those times that you can't come with me, love.
I shall miss you".

"Not there to make tea" she said with a stiff smile and tearful eyes.

"Have I ever told you that I love your tea?"

She squeezed his hand, smiled and nodded knowingly.

"Go now, my man and come back safely"

The small children gathered around his leggings as he leaned forward and kissed Mary.

He patted each on the head, bent and lifted his roll, slung it over one shoulder, then turned and strode to the water's edge.

The small canoe already contained William Dunnett, Boatman,
John Ross, Middleman and the Steersman, Mr James.

As they paddled into midstream, Peter waved at the diminishing figures and then faced forwards. In just a few miles they would meet Mr Tomison and head for the Churchill River.

The crew talked over the top of Peter's head as though he wasn't there.

"Not very sure about this guide" said Dunnett. "He got a good deal out of this."

"What was the deal?" asked Ross.

"Pint of powder, pound of shot, 20 balls and three feet of tobacco"
He spat into the fast moving waters.

"I'd have taken you for that!"

James and Ross laughed.

"Yeah. You mean you'd have got us lost for that!" joked James.

Peter smiled, said nothing.

"I think that's the mouth of the Reindeer River over there" said James, nodding across the heaving water.

"And what do we have here?" said Dunnett, pointing to the left hand bank. "Somebody waving. Trying to attract our attention".

"Move in beyond musket shot, William, if you please" said Peter, kneeling on one knee and shading his eyes.

The figure was an Indian. He shouted something.

"He come from Deer Lake settlement" said their guide. "He sent to take us in to Mr Spence"

"Right. He can hop in and take us on. Let Mr Tomison know. I'll be taking some observations till we get there" said Fidler, opening his roll and waterproofs.

"Pleased to see you, pleased to see you" said Mr Spence at Deer Lake settlement after greeting Mr Tomison.

" Heard a lot about you Mr Fidler. Never met before. Do come in. Yes. All of you. Do come in"

"I've already fixed a meal for everyone so make yourselves at home."

He hooked his arm through Peter's and led him towards one of the larger cabins.

"Got some mail for you, too Mr Fidler"

"Call me Peter"

"Right Peter. Thanks. Where was I? Oh yes. Letter from Mr Auld"

Peter sat at the long table alongside Tomison and opened the bulky letter.

It contained an abstract of David Thompson's journey through the same area, including Athabascow Lake.

"You won't be able to paddle to the north of the lake . " said Spence. "It's frozen for about 140 miles. I think we should have a word with your guide and see if we can get any useful suggestions"

Spence, Tomison and Fidler went outside. The guide was squatting with several other Indians around a fire against a lean-to teepee.

He listened to them and nodded, then stood.

"I think we leave lake, portage short way, then come back to lake later. More down lake."

"Sounds a decent solution" said Spence. "What do you reckon?"

"I've just been reading some of Davy Thompson's records. Seems there's a river called the Chee or Canoe River along the way which might be suitable." Peter said to both Tomison and Spence. "If we can pick that up, it may be a suitable route."

"Not know Chee River" said their guide.

"Well, it could be called the Canoe River?"

"Not know Canoe River" insisted their guide.

"Perhaps it's called something else. If we move to a clean piece of sand, I'll draw it for you"

"Not know Something Else River"

135

"I should give up, Peter" said Spence."I recognise the symptoms, don't you? He doesn't want to go no matter what it's called."

"My friend. He good guide. He know Chee River. Be guide for me"

Their guide spoke to an Indian still squatting near his feet. The man grunted, stood, picked up his rolled belongings and walked directly to the nearest canoe.

"It'll be a bit squashed for room in that small canoe, but we'll manage" Peter turned to the ex-guide.

"You'll have to share your payment with your friend" he said.

The man nodded and told the new guide.

As the first guide had said, there was little life in the woods.

Peter's canoe went alongside Tomison.

"I'd like to try and generate a bit of life along this route, if there is any to be had"

"How do you propose doing that, Peter"

"My idea is to make some pretty hefty fires at intervals until somebody turns up to investigate"

Tomison looked dubious but thought for a moment.

"OK Try it out and see what happens." He sniffed.

"But try not to set the whole damn lot on fire!"

Peter smiled. It was about as near as Tomison got to swearing.

At intervals, he went ashore with one or other of his crew to make large fires.

And so they travelled, mile after mile, but there was no sign of life.

The first guide seemed agitated.

" No like this country heap much" he suddenly blurted out.

William Dunnett came over to Peter by the camp fire that night.

"I think we're gonna have to keep an eye on those guides. 'Specially the first one. He's not unpacked anything and I reckon he could be away like a deer before morning. If you feel the same way, I'll fix up a watch with me and some of the other guys to keep an eye on them both"

Peter nodded. "Fine William. But don't tire yourself out. It's still going to be a long day tomorrow."

Dunnett nodded and walked away.

The guide looked sullen next morning when the canoes started the next leg of the journey which led them to a very large, unnamed Lake.

"I think I'll call this Lake Wollaston after one of one of the Hudson's

Bay Committee." he said thoughtfully, balancing to take bearings. "It might earn us a better pension!"

The men laughed and Peter directed them along the eastern side of the lake.

"This is a fairly large bay "said James. "Probably deserves a name of its own"

"How about Dunnitt Bay ?" said William.

"Or in Cree language 'He-who-sets-fire-to-forest-and-frightens -life-out-of-bird -and-beast!" quipped John.

"Not too far out, John" said William. He turned half-towards Peter.

"Why not 'Peter Fidler's Bay? Everybody else has something named after them? Mackenzie River, Thompson Bay, Ross Bay, Turnor Rapids"

"Anything to keep the peace" said Peter with a red face. "I'll record it as that, but you can bet that somebody at York or London will rename it"

And so it became known as 'Peter Fidler's Bay'.

As they continued their journey, stopping for food or rest, the brief conversations erupted.

"I think I'm right in saying that you've been along here before, ain't you Peter?"

"Yes. Some years ago. Slightly different route and approach. David Thompson was also along here about 11 years ago. I came with Turnor."

He picked up his waterproof record pack and looked at some sketches.

"I was only thinking about that a few minutes ago, William. Not far along here, about five miles I guess, I marked a pine tree. 1791 I think it was. We'll have a rest near there and I'll go and see if I can find it"

Less than an hour later, they pulled into the bank.

Peter helped pull the two canoes ashore, then after informing Tomison, he walked a few hundred yards to a small knoll. There were the remains of an old pine tree that had broken off about four feet from the ground. The detached trunk had rotted and was covered in lichen.

He wrote in his diary " Found the pine tree I marked in 1791, but it has fallen down".

At the place where they had set up camp, they were pestered by millions of sandflies. Every time they tried to cook food, the air was filled with them.

They were pleased to leave that spot and leave for the clean openness of the river.

"Those damm flies were driving me crazy last night" growled James.

"Sounded like goddam rain, bashing agin the tent!"

Day after day they travelled on Peter constantly taking bearings, sketching and making observations. They stopped at intervals to rest, make camp and pursue some exploratory side journeys.

The first guide came to Peter.

"White man follow. Hide river bend. Watch us". He unfolded his arms and pointed. There was nothing to be seen but Peter knew that there would be someone, as the guide had said.

"Thank you Lone Feather, I will tell our men".

"My friend now good guide. Yes? I leave. Go home. Come back. You pay me then. OK?"

Peter nodded and put out a hand. The Indian took it.

"Thank you Lone Feather. You have been very good guide. Go in peace. You will be paid when you return"

The next evening they returned to camp. It was a disaster area. The goods were scattered everywhere, food left open to the elements, spoiled by two Northwesters, Boucher and McDougall who had visited and wrecked it. They had been sent to follow the Hudson's Bay group to discover what they were doing and where they were going.

The explorers spent some time around the fringes of Wollaston Lake.

On the final return journey, Fidler slipped on some rocks, trapped a foot and tore off a toe nail. His foot swelled badly and he limped back to the canoe in great pain.

At the edge of camp, that evening, a figure appeared. It groaned and fell to the ground near the fire. William and James approached the figure. An Indian, Lone Feather, who had been badly beaten. Two ribs were broken.

The tended him and listened to his story. He had been on his way to meet them and collect his payment when he had been ambushed and beaten by two Northwesters, one of whom he recognised as La Roche with a colleague.

He refused to stay. Peter paid him and offered to take him along, but he refused saying that he would go home. That night he left.

"I think it's time to push on more swiftly" said Peter thoughtfully. "I've done what I set out to do on this leg. We've visited Nelson House area and are now back to the Churchill River".

He looked around at the tense faces.

"Tomorrow morning then?"

They nodded.

They reached Churchill Factory having been away several months. Peter had collected an impressive dossier of courses, directions, sketches, maps, descriptions.

William helped him to sort them out .

" I've only just found out that we recorded sixty-three portages between Churchill and Isle-A-La-Crosse!" he said. "I wouldn't have known if I hadn't looked at your maps!"

He smoothed a sheet of leather with his hand.

"Makes mi' legs ache just thinking about it! Where are you sending this information, Peter?"

"The completed report is for Mr Auld, but he intends to send it on to England, to the Committee"

"They should be pleased with this, then" said William

"It means a trip to York Factory in September. Then I'm to move on to Swan River House in October." explained Peter.

He turned and looked through the door into the distance.

"Time flies. It's 1807 already and almost eleven years since I was there before."

He sighed, smiled and carried on sorting the records.

Linklater was returning to Swan River House. His breath curled behind him as he manhandled the hand sled on his own, along and down frozen embankments, through decorated trees.

"Weel, look what we have here! A wee man with a big sled!"

"Looks as though he might need help, with that stuff" said another voice.

Linklater spun round.

Two fur-clad figures looked down at him. Two guns pointed at his stomach.

Linklater recognised the first speaker. J D Campbell, a Northwester who had been reported in the region recently. It was he who had destroyed Fidler's gardens at Green Lake and burned down Auld's Fort built in 1799.

"Hiya Mr Campbell" Greeted Linklater. "Didn't expect to see you out here"

"So, ye didn't expect to see me out here did you, little man!"

Campbell came near. The other man raised his gun.

"And what have we bundled up on yon sled? Looks like furs, to me. Don't

139

you know that all the furs round here are ours? Has naebody told ye?"

Without warning, he struck Linklater in the ribs with the butt of his gun. Linklater's knees sagged and he grunted loudly with pain.

"Now. I think ye'll have tae take a message to Mr Auld. Tell him thanks for helping us this far with our furs".

Linklater was standing, doubled-up from the blow. Campbell leaned forward, grabbed the frame of each snowshoe and pulled. Linklater's feet shot into the air and he fell heavily against the side of a nearby tree..

"Gimme a hand with this" Campbell ordered his colleague.

The accomplice slung his gun around his neck, came forward and the two men hauled away the sled.

Auld had begun to experience at first hand the viciousness of the Northwesters. He wrote to York House

"Nothing less than armed men and numbers not less than the Canadians are needed to increase our returns".

Colin Robertson resigned from the North West Company and joined Hudson's Bay Company.

Auld and he went to London in 1809.

Auld rose from the dining table.

A servant pulled out his chair from behind him.

"We'd better go inside, Colin"

"Aye. You're right William. It will be the first time for me. You'll never believe it but I'm nervous!"

Auld laughed.

"I've stopped feeling like that now, Colin. I realise that I'm useful to them and their business. So will you be. And that's why they value us. If they don't listen at least to some of what we say, then their dividends are going to vanish."

Colin seemed uncomfortable in his frilled shirt and waistcoat.

The meeting room was full and smoky. A chatter filled the air.

Servants stood at intervals, inscrutable, against the dark oak panelling.

Auld and Robertson were sat several places from the Chairman to whose right sat a tall, broad-shouldered man with a long aquiline nose and disdainful expression.

The Chairman banged his gavel. The talking ceased and all members looked towards him intently.

"Good evening gentlemen. Without any more ado, I shall introduce you to our principal speaker this evening, Mr Andrew Wedderburn. We also have in our midst Mister William Auld, known to you all and Mr Colin Robertson, late of the North West Company. Mr Wedderburn?

Wedderburn stood languidly. His clothing was elegantly tailored.

When he spoke, his voice was deep and strong.

"I am flattered that the Committee has chosen to invite me to share my proposals with you. Before I do, I shall remind you that our profits for the past two years have declined seriously. "

He leaned on one extended arm, with the other behind his back.

"We estimate the loss of trade in the vicinity of nineteen thousand pounds"

There was an intake of breath around the table,

"My recommendations will not be easy, and it is unlikely that they will be totally painless"

He looked around and a smile creased his mouth.

"At least, not totally painless to our competitors".

Chuckles and some sniggers.

"Mr Auld" he nodded politely towards William, who dropped his head once in acknowledgement, "Wrote to us some weeks ago. I shall quote one of his remarks. He said ' Nothing less than armed men and numbers not less than the Canadians are needed to increase our returns'. Those are practical words, gentlemen. Words of wisdom. Words from a trusted Master in the region.

I agree with him. We are outnumbered. Our men have been instructed to behave lawfully in the teeth of lawlessness. Not to rock the canoe, if I may refresh the cliche."

He picked up a glass. A servant stepped across quickly and poured a small measure of claret.

He sipped once, delicately, put down the glass, stretched to his full height and leaned forward again.

"We must improve our communications by making the region more accessible. The way to do that is by making a Northern Region and a Southern Region. The areas are outlined on the maps provided so kindly by our Surveyor Mr Peter Fidler and are available for your perusal after the meeting.

I propose that we appoint Mr Auld as Master of the Northern region based on York Factory.

In addition, I should like to propose using the expertise of Mr Robertson

141

to open up Lake Athabaska again, where resistance by the North West Company is most violent.

If we are not careful, we shall lose our traders. I propose therefore that we pay our Chief Traders a salary plus bonus. Poor performers will be released, 'economy' will be the watchword. Some of the older employees will be 'let go' "

His proposals continued for another half hour.

At the end he said "We have many brave, loyal and skilful employees. The maps to which I alluded were produced by one of them, Peter Fidler. He is now 40 years of age and may one day become the Chief Trader. I feel that it will be an encouragement to them all if we should commend him for his performance"

A clatter of applause punctuated by "Here, here" greeted the suggestion.

Wedderburn sat. From the buzz of conversation around the table it was obvious that his suggestions had been received favourably.

"Mr Auld?" said the Chairman with raised eyebrows.

Auld stood. The undercurrent of sound faded to silence.

Raising his head he said " Three years ago, I maligned Mr Fidler. In my report, and from a position of ignorance, I referred to his 'spaniel-like behaviour'. Now, I regret deeply having make such a comment. I served with him after my remarks He is, in fact, cool, courageous, talented. However, one of my first jobs must be to send him, yet again, to a trading post which suffers badly from attacks by the Northwesters. To Isle-A-La-Crosse. If anyone can rebuild it and defend it, then it will be Peter Fidler"

He looked at the ceiling then back to the table.

"I am aware what I am having to do. There are about 26 Canadians and their supporters. Fidler will have only eight."

He sat down abruptly to a room of silence.

Peter with his small team of 8 men, Mary and the children, all sharing four canoes set off on 9th June 1810 through the rapids of Churchill River and on to Isle-A-La-Crosse where he had been instructed to take command.

He expected trouble, probably of the kind they had been subjected to at Nottingham House.

But his mind was full of local scenes and sights with occasional pleasurable thoughts about his rise in salary to 100 pounds a year and confirmation of the title of Surveyor.

He and Mary were delighted at the letter of commendation from the Committee in London and even more delighted at the friendly and understanding letter from William Auld, his new boss.

One phrase stuck in his mind "You are considered by all to be the best man to face up to the challenges of the future"

He looked guiltily around, hoping that he hadn't voiced the thought out loud. He cleared his throat and sang a tuneless ditty under his breath to cover it if he had. Mary waved one hand from the following canoe. He waved back.

His men pulled the canoes out of the river. He walked towards the fort, puzzled by its strange shape. Then the answer came like a kick in the chest.

The Northwesters had built a watchtower at his gate, manned by armed men.

Worse was to greet him.

At the base of the tower stood Bully Black, one pistol in a chest holster and another at his waist, talking to Campbell the old adversary from Reindeer Lake. A third man was with them, sporting bandoliers of ammunition, two pistols, and two Bowie knives.

"Hey, Fidler. Fancy meeting you here!" bawled Black, feet astride, hands on hips.

"So you're Fidler, hey" said the unknown man "Don't look much to me, Mr Campbell"

"May I introduce Peter Skeen Ogden, Mr Fidler. You don't need any introduction to your old friend Mr Black, I take it!" said Campbell, smirking..

Peter made no reply. He looked around from water to fort.

Campbell had expect some other response. His face darkened with anger. He muttered something to Black who reached for the chest pistol, cocked it, aimed at the Company's weather vane and fired. The beaver spun round with part of its tail missing.

Peter's men froze at the edge of the river, unsure of the situation. Peter turned and walked into the fort. They picked up whatever they could and hurried after him. Several Indians standing by impassively moved back several paces.

None offered to help.

By the third day, Peter and his men had a good idea of the situation as it was developing.

143

He called his men together into the trading room and posted sentries two near the windows and a third towards the gate.

"Well, lads, we can see what Campbell and his ruffians are up to. Not a single Indian has been near since we arrived. They are threatened with punishment worse than death if they even speak to us so they are staying well away."

"Can't blame the poor devils" said a man at the front. "I wouldn't talk to me if I didn't have to !"

Cracked smiles appeared.

Thomas, the Storeman said from the back "We'll be running outta grub pretty soon. I tried to catch some fish but they stole the fishing line and nets this morning".

John in charge of firewood, a tall bearded man in tartan shirt spoke up." Like I told you, they carried away the firewood so we's gonna have a lotta trouble with the cold if we ain't careful like"

"Jesus! Here comes Pat. Looks as though somebody rough-housed him" said one of the sentries.

Faces turned to the door as a tall, wiry figure with a shock of red hair stumbled into their midst. They held him while a keg was fetched for him to sit on. His nose was bleeding, an egg sized lump decorated his head. His left eyes was closing rapidly.

Mary pushed her way through with a small pan of water and a piece of clean rag.

"Sonsabitches" he said angrily. "Two of 'em jumped me as I walked down to the gate to see what they were up to. I coulda beat the pair of 'em but a t'ird one came from behind and tripped me. By the skirts of Saint Patrick, when I get 'em I'll knock the livin' daylights out of 'em"

He grimaced, gave a gasp of pain and spat into the pan. "They've even loosened one'a me best teeth!"

"Sure, an that's not all" he went on before anyone could interrupt. "The Yank says that nobody is to leave the House else he'll kill them himself. Sure and I believe him. He's a murderous dog"

"OK " said Peter. "Don't put yourselves at risk. I'll do what I can about food, but we may have to tighten our belts now and again. I'll pass on any news later. Thanks for coming. Just try to get on with things as though nothing has happened. Easier said than done, I know"

Next morning, Peter sent for Sutherland and Thomas the Storeman.

"I'm going over to the Northwester fort to see Mr Henry and enquire whether can use their Blacksmith for a couple of jobs. I want you two to take what you need and drop over the back wall. Mr Sutherland, you will go out to Green Lake taking the nearest canoe and three men. Set up a trading post as best you can.

Thomas, I want you to lay as many nets as possible. With luck we might get away with it".

Peter strolled unconcernedly through the gate and towards the enemy's fort. Several shots ploughed into the ground around him but he tried not to show his fear. Loud laughter came from their watchtower behind him.

He was met at the gate by Robert Henry.

"Waddya want, Fidler! Thought you'd been told to stay put?"

"Good morning Robert. Wondered if I could borrow your Blacksmith for a short while. Need a couple of jobs done that our man can't do"

Henry looked at him fixedly.

"Goddam it! You're up to something, Fidler. And the answer's no! Ain't you got the message yet?"

He walked away.

That night, Black circled Hudson's Bay fort. Along with others, he shrieked and fired his weapons. Few of the occupants slept. Mary, Peter and the children huddled together.

The following morning was quiet. But activity broke out at the Northwesters fort in the afternoon. Canoes sped along the river in several directions. Sutherland had been missed and scouts were sent to find his trail.

They also found the nets and two Northwesters, Clark and McDougal destroyed them.

No reports about Sutherland came back either from him or the Northwesters.

In August, three of the partners of the North West Company John G McTavish, John McGillivray and Simon Fraser, visited the region.

Black and Ogden continued their antics during the visit.

At the end of Autumn, Black and Ogden were reported entering the fort. Peter met them in the yard.

"Get outta my way, ye goddam prissy little Englishman" snarled Black, pushing Peter.

"Get out of here. You aren't welcome" said Fidler angrily.

145

"Well, now. What have we here? Look at this little cockerel" gloated Ogden

"George! Shut the west gates" Fidler ordered.

George hurried away and with a couple of men closed the west gates.

"So, Fidler, what in hell are ya gonna do now" taunted Ogden.

Black shoved Fidler on the chest again, so that Peter almost fell.

Fidler looked around, picked up a nearby stick and hit Black across the face with it. Then again, twice more.

Black staggered back, holding his face, stunned at the attack. Blood seeped through his fingers. Bellowing like a bull and holding one arm up to protect his face, he leapt forwards and grabbed the stick from Fidler.

He struck, shattering Fidler's thumb.

Peter staggered backwards, holding the blood-dripping hand.

Ogden suddenly awoke, drew a heavy knife, struck at Fidler's back.

The dagger tore through Peter's jacket and pierced his skin, but did not penetrate far.

With a cry of rage, Black smashed the stick across Fidler's back. It broke in half. Black threw the remains into Fidler's face and kicked his legs from under him.

Ogden joined in and the two men kicked and punched Fidler as he rolled around trying to protect himself.

Black stood back and drew a pistol as Ogden continued kicking. He held the gun by the barrel and pistol-whipped Peter around the head and shoulders.

The Northwesters grew tired of their actions, delivered final blows and swaggered out of the gates.

Before leaving, Black turned around and shouted

"Sonsabitches ye'll not get a goddam skin from this place, mark my words!"

They left.

The yard was filled with Hudson's Bay men but none had gone to Peter's aid!

They lifted him gently and without conversation and took him into his quarters.

Mary ran out, crying, to hold his hand.

Food became very scarce. James Isbister was sent to hunt partridge but his movements were reported to Black and Ogden who lay in wait for him.

The beating they administered was savage and they smashed his gun, threatening to break his arms next time they saw him.

James returned in great pain, crying with shame and humiliation.

Fidler recorded in 1811 that all these attacks were performed in deadly earnest. The Northwesters were never drunk when they did them.

Black and Ogden seem to have been psychopaths who took great pleasure in the pain, hurt and fear that they inflicted. .

Yet, in January, Black and Ogden came visiting, completely out of character.

"Listen Fidler, we're gonna take letters to the Saskatchewan River post. If you want, we'll deliver some for you, provided you send one of your guys along with us" said Ogden. "Whaddya say?"

Peter was surprised but stayed calm.

"Sounds a good idea to me. Let me get my stuff together and pick somebody and I'll let you know in a couple of hours .OK?"

They nodded and left.

Fidler had written a number of letters to Mr Bird at Edmonton House, but he wrote an additional, most secret letter.

He selected his messenger, took his jacket and had the letter, bound in oilcloth, sewn into the lining. It told Bird that they intended to vacate this post in the spring and asked Bird to supply them with pemmican for the outward journey as they had no food.

The message reached Bird safely and he wrote a reply which returned in February.

"I am unable to provide you with meat as we have had a poor season. You may be interested to know that David Thompson was prevented by the Piegan Indians from crossing the Rocky Mountains at the head of the Saskatchewan River.

Additionally, the Muddy River Indians massacred an American Officer and his command near the source of the Missouri River and scalped them all. The Indians rifled their bodies and came away with 110 American three-dollar bank notes. They sold them for very little to the Canadian Master at the Northwesters House in Saskatchewan."

Perhaps food for the mind if not for the body.

Even more surprisingly, Campbell visited. He asked if Peter could spare some turnip seed. He was given turnip seed together with Windsor beans, runner beans, parsley and carrot seeds.

Black and Ogden also visited. They made small talk, were no trouble

147

and left.

Fishing continued whenever possible. Their most cunning fisherman was a man named Kirkness who quite often, with a poacher's skill, avoided the Northwesters.

But he was caught on the water.

They told him that his wife was having an affair with one of their men and offered him rum.

Kirkness, aflame with jealousy and liquor, went home and beat his wife. That night, she ran away and joined the Northwesters.

Next day and for several days following, he went to the Northwesters fort to plead with her to return.

He didn't fish and so Mary volunteered.

Peter thought about it and consulted Mary.

"Have you any suggestions, Sweetheart?"

she said thoughtfully

" Very little harm has been offered the women or small children. So, I can handle the nets and the fishing for the time being"

Peter placed both arms around her and rested his cheek on her shiny black hair.

"There has never been a single moment when I couldn't rely on you and your judgement, Mary. It was a wonderful day when I met you ".

He kissed her tenderly.

"Still, I know that the older children can be in danger. Charles, at the tender age of 12, has already been fired at on several occasions. He was lucky last time to have escaped injury."

"Our women from both camps will continue to talk. I should be able to collect useful talk ." Said Mary

Indeed she was. She told Peter that the Kirkness woman was being held against her will.

Kirkness had becoming a morbid, drunken liability.

Sutherland returned.

"You and I will go over and try to persuade Kirkness' woman to return." said Peter.

Black and Ogden leaned over the watchtower rail.

"So you've come back, eh, Sutherland! Don't think we dinna know what you've been up to"

"We've come to talk to Mr Henry" said Peter.

148

"Well, is that so? I'm terrible sorry, but ye'll have tae speak wi' me, Fidler. What is it ye want?"

"If we must, then we must. We want to talk to Kirkness' wife"

Black turned gleefully to Ogden.

"Listen to the English gentleman! Kirkness' wife! He must mean the slut that sleeping around with everybody!"

He turned to the men below him. "That's not Kirkness' wife. She was his woman and now she's somebody else's woman! Anybody else's woman! And she's satisfied by the men she finds here, not the old women over there" he pointed with his chin.

The scar across his cheek still looked red and angry.

"We'd still like to ask her ourselves".

"Would ye now! Would ye indeed.!" He turned to Ogden again who seemed to be enjoying the spectacle.

With an exaggerated bow from the waist he said "Mr Ogden. Would ye be so kind as to fetch milady out here?. These English gentlemen would love tae discuss matters with her"

Ogden tittered and slid into the guardroom. A slap followed by a scream, then the dishevelled woman was shoved on to the balcony.

Peter looked up at her ."I've come to ask you to return to your husband, Mrs Kirkness. He admits that he made a mistake and is very sorry. He misses you very much. Will you consider it, please?"

Ogden grabbed her long hair and waved a heavy knife.

"She's goin' nowhere, Fidler. If she is, she's not taking her nose and ears, 'cos I'll cut 'em off!"

The woman screamed and cowered down, tears running freely down a dirty face.

"I don't think we can help at the moment, Peter. Let's go and talk about it"

They left and returned to the post.

James met them in the trading room.

"Kirkness has gone" he said. "He ran out of the gates with some belongings just after you got back".

"Damm!" said Sutherland. "That's twice as much to worry about now"

It was only three weeks later that a panting Kirkness reappeared at the cabin.

Peter sent for him immediately and posted extra lookouts.

149

"Tell me your story, Mr Kirkness" he said. Mary with Sutherland stood in the background.

"I thought I'd get her back if I went over there" he said brokenly.

"Did you get her back?"

"No. No I didn't! " Kirkness put both hands up to his face.

"The bastards beat me. Then they beat her. They wouldn't let us be together at all. Never! But I talked to her through the wall. She was goin' to come with me but they caught her. I think they took her into Campbell's room until she said she wasn't goin' to leave. That's when I took off."

He looked up.

"Sorry for all this, I am Mr Fidler. And I've had a bellyfull o' them. I'm 'fraid for her now. They said they'd let all the men rape her if I left."

He burst into tears and cradled his face. Sobs retched out of him

"An' now I've done it. I've left. She don't deserve all this"

There was little they could do.

Fidler's group packed and prepared to leave for Churchill on 4th June. The weather was hot and calm

Kirkness' woman appeared briefly, at the watchtower balcony, without clothes, showing many bruises. Three naked men appeared, one waving a jug of rum. She screamed and they dragged her back into the room.

Their final memory of the trading post was a column of smoke as the Northwesters set fire to it.

The same fate befell Sutherland's post at Green Lake.

The attempt to dig-in at Athabaska had failed

Mary was pregnant. On 27th June as they traversed Chalk Portage, a daughter was born named Mary.

CHAPTER 10

WAR against NORTHWESTERS and METIS

(1812 - 1815)

Wedderburn meant his new policy to be far reaching

"William, you are appointed to the Northern department as proposed. That covers Winnipeg and Saskatchewan."

William Auld nodded.

"And shall we be able to stretch our muscles a little more?"he queried.

Wedderburn snipped the end of a Cuban cigar. He looked across Hyde Park, bathed in sunlight.

Several women riders rode sidesaddle, jauntily, along its edge. Small children bowled hoops whilst nannies pushed prams, chatted, avoided puddles and horse manure.

"We expect you to defend like men the property that is entrusted to you. If any persons shall presume to make a forcible attack upon you, then you have arms in your hands"

He turned to face Auld.

"I believe I make myself clear? I shall of course put these instructions in writing, later.".

Auld nodded again "You do indeed and thank you. Now I can plan to take Fidler, Snodie and some other men to York Factory in July and make preparations".

"I want the Red River region settled. It will provide an abundance of furs and the timber we need for other purposes, yet to be determined"

"Have you thought who the likely settlers will be?" asked Auld.

"I have, of course. There are several options. One which comes easily to mind is the request from many of our Scots employees who would like to settle permanently overseas. I think that we can offer them 30 acres of land after three year contracts. You can send Fidler to survey the properties. Yes?"

He moved away from the window and sat at a large ornate desk with rococo edging, curved mahogany legs and polished leather surface.

His cigar smoke curled upwards in a solid column.

"My brother-in-law, Lord Selkirk, a very wealthy and charitable gentleman, may be persuaded to finance the Red River colony. You doubtless will be aware that he started a colony of dispossessed Scots in Prince Edward Island which is surviving rather well"

Auld looked at him.

He was about to say "And one at Baldoon, which didn't" but held his tongue.

"Is he not a new shareholder?" he asked instead.

"He is, but he is reluctant to tie himself down by becoming a member of the Committee. A wise decision. I believe his talents lie elsewhere. He agrees with me that Red River settlement is both desirable and practical".

Red River Settlers

Auld didn't agree, but said nothing, except to Peter Fidler when they met in York some weeks later.

"He has appointed Miles Macdonell as the over-all Governor of the new Colony. I breathed a sigh of relief, I can tell you. It's bad enough tackling something impossible that you like doing! It's worse tackling it when you don't like doing it!".

He stopped, repeated to himself what he had just said then laughed.

"I'm sure that's very philosophical Peter. Pity that only you and I can savour it!"

"What happened to Colin Robertson?"

"Well, he and Macdonell have gone off to the north of Scotland to recruit potential settlers. I was told before I left that Alexander MacKenzie and Simon McGillivray were also campaigning in that area. Should be interesting!. Robertson sent a message just before I left to say that they had about 200 volunteers to report to Stornoway for embarkation"

Peter was about to return to England after twenty three years away on service with the Company.

Bolsover, Derbyshire, England seemed very desirable at the moment. More so than Red River settlers. His mother, brother Joseph and his sister Sarah were still in Bolsover and, he hoped, would have been informed well in advance about his return.

The ship was late.

They met the ship's boats as they landed. The vessel itself looked battered. Sails were being hauled down for repair.

"Mr Auld, sir?"

A Company Petty Officer saluted and held out a bulky envelope".

"Thank you" said Auld, turning it over in his hands. "News from the Committee, Peter. Let's go inside and see what we have. "

When opened they told nothing new. Confirmation was given that Auld would be replaced by Miles Macdonell and it was hoped that the Governor-elect would be able to feed the extra 105 settlers to be landed.

Auld's face darkened as he read on.

"MacKenzie and McGillivray beat us to it, the scoundrels! Only 105 of the volunteer 200 turned up at Stornoway!."

Whilst Auld was reading his mail, Peter had been talking with one of the ship's officers.

"He tells me that these are the fore-runners of another batch to be sent next year. They've had troubles galore. It's been worse than the Civil War, he says! Irish have fought among themselves and then joined to fight the northern Scots.

There were some cases of scurvy which didn't quieten the panic."

Auld looked up with a haunted look.

"It's too late to send them on to Red River now. They'd neve make it and even if they ever got there, which I doubt, they'd never be able to look after themselves."

He looked around at the immigrants as they clustered in groups nearby. He heaved a sigh.

"I shall have to make arrangements to keep them here until next year. A daunting prospect, indeed. I envy you your holiday, Peter".

Return To Bolsover, Derbyshire, England

A westerly breeze had followed the coach from Chesterfield to Bolsover, pushing ahead occasional dust from clouds kicked up by the wheels.

A film of dust was sprinkled on his coat and on the clothes of the other three passengers. He loosened the thick leather strap securing the window, and leaned out. Dust flew into his eyes as the coach jolted along.

Several hundred yards ahead he could make out a small group of people in front of a solitary house by the roadside.

His mother's house! He felt great excietment .

In the middle distance, Bolsover Castle lay, long, indefatigable.

It was twenty three years since he last saw his mother.

His heart pounded. She would be a much older lady now. He had missed her best years, departed as a boy and returned as a man of means.

He reached for his hand luggage and top hat, swaying with the coach as it slowed to a halt.

The one out-rider released his baggage and passed it down as the group of strangers surrounded him. Then he saw them all. The years fell away.

"Mother!" he croaked and she held out her arms.

Sarah, his sister, a matronly woman, with Joseph his brother. A couple of children he had yet to learn about and a couple of neighbours with wide grins, shaking hands.

Willing hands collected his carpet bags and belongings, hoisted them, took them indoors.

The driver clicked his teeth, shook the reins and the two horses moved away towards town.

Peter resettled very quickly. He walked for miles around the area. Views were different. No endless forests, violent rivers, vicious winters. The countryside had been manicured for a thousand years.

Hedges were green, fruits were plentiful, fields cultivated.

Within a radius of twenty miles there were thousands of people living in towns whose names he had used overseas. Bolsover, Chesterfield, Mansfield, Nottingham, even Sutton Mill, his birthplace.

The castle still towered above the area, long, grey powerful, dominating.

Peter walked up the hill towards it, one day and stood on a piece of undeveloped ground nearby. His father had died, stipulating that Peter must return home within a year of the death to be able to claim against his will. That condition had been satisfied.

It was then that he decided to build a stone house for his mother. On this piece of ground. Level with the castle.

He contacted builders, took estimates, commissioned one group to go ahead. It cost 400 pounds, a good quality house, and he named it "Hudson's Bay House.

He made arrangements to maintain the house in his own name, with the intention of retiring there with his family after leaving Hudson's Bay service.

He kept a notebook of costs relating to the building of the house,

155

including descriptions of materials, tradesmen's bills unaware that one day the records would be valuable property themselves, retained in the Public Archives of Manitoba.

He had been missing Mary and the children for some time. He now realised that he missed the very things he had been glad to leave. The forests, rivers, new sights and sounds, challenges.

He glanced at his waist. It looked heavier than when he'd arrived.

His time here was spent too lazily, even though he had been involved daily with the house building and moving.

He had been to several cricket matches, visited the few local 'pubs' and listened to the stories of men, with whom, as children, he had not been able to play.

His education at The Grange and his father's occupation had not given him much opportunity to make friends among neighbour's children.

Although he fell easily back into the local accent and idiom, he felt obliged to reduce his vocabulary and only answered direct questions concerning his life overseas.

Several men of his own age had travelled, in the army on the continent and in the Americas. They had something in common, but it was not with him.

Early in June, he heard a horse and trap pull into the yard, a gruff voice, then a brief clackety as a horse left. His mother brought a small mail pouch into the lounge, brushed it with her pinafore and laid it on the table.

He opened the pocket and took out a sealed envelope from the Company.

It asked that he terminate his leave and return to London for a briefing concerning new proposals for the Red River colony. They seemed to consider it a foregone conclusion that he would do so.

A meeting had been arrange with Lord Selkirk at the Company offices in London in the middle of June and a berth had been booked on an outgoing company ship.

He could be better used overseas.

When his mother was settled in the new house, he left for London.

The ship arrived at York Factory after eight tumultuous weeks at sea. Once again, Irish and Scots had fallen out not only among themselves and each other, but with the expedition leader, Owen Keveny.

He stepped ashore with Peter Fidler on 26th August 1812.

"I can hardly believe it" he said looking around in astonishment."I recognise a number of these people. They should have been at Red River last year! I'll have a word and see what's happened"

The result was not reassuring.

"Some of these are setting off tomorrow. Another group left a couple of days ago. It looks as though Mr Auld, Mr Macdonell and other fur traders have fallen out about the settlement".

Peter nodded. He knew that Auld had not been in favour of the settlement, but chose not to say nothing.

"And in addition" went on Keveny, "Only 19 men went with Macdonell. Now, the others don't want to go! Can you believe it!"

Peter moved into his quarters then took a stroll to get a better idea of the problems. He was still wearing his English clothing and was treated as a gentleman rather than a fur trader.

He went out and met Keveny in the noisy, smoky tavern.

"I think they lack some positive leadership" he said, sipping at his tankard of whiskey. "So. Tomorrow, we'll organise some boats, probably into three groups, and set off at intervals of a day. I can take three men with me in a canoe and move from one group to the other to keep them going."

He looked around at a couple of loud, red-faced groups of potential settlers.

Hudson's Bay Company sailing ships
Prince Albert and Prince Rupert off Mansel Island, Hudson's Bay.
J. Spurling (Provincial Archives P445)

"It will be hard for a lot of them. They don't look as though they have the physique for such a difficult journey. Then, neither did I when younger but I managed!"

He left Keveny to his job as expedition leader responsible for informing his groups of intended action.

The 11 boats sailed as planned. Fidler moved backwards and forwards between the three groups, encouraging and helping them .

He wrote in his diary

"Several are quite useless for some time by the constant walking and great fatigue they undergo".

He drew up to the first group, stood balancing and shouted

"You will see Oxford House within the hour. Mr Sinclair will make you welcome. Pull your boats ashore. The rest will follow over the next day or two".

William Sinclair, the Chief Factor made them all very welcome and the three groups breathed sighs of relief at being off the river.

"Miles Macdonell went through a while ago, Peter" he said over dinner. "I was able to present them with a year old bull and a heifer. I think they've called them Adam and Eve". He roared with laughter.

"There aren't any other cattle there, before them, William" said Peter, smiling."So it's a good choice of names!"

"How much longer do you expect to take with these tenderfeet, Peter?" asked Heney, looking serious.

"They're not too bad, really. Just unfit for this kind of travel at the moment. They'll be fitter by the time they get there, no doubt. Most of them won't stray very far from the settlement in future, I expect. But that's not answering your question, William."

He thought for a moment as he cut the moose meat into small pieces.

"About seven weeks from now, barring accidents. Late October"

"I hope so, Peter. Winter is barking at our heels now."

It was October 27th 1812 when they reached the area designated for the settlement.

No arrangements had been made to receive them.

Macdonell had moved with his group to Pembina about sixty miles upstream. Peter urged on his tired group to follow them.

They were welcomed by the Factor, Hugh Heney.

"You'll love the view!" he told Peter and pointed across the river as light faded.

"Northwesters. Fort Gibraltar. Your old friend John Wills!".

He put another couple of logs on the fire and crossed his feet on a small stool.

"Macdonell is across there, now"

He noted Peter's look of surprise.

"Yup. Seems to be very friendly with them. He's even talked to them about his new settlement and his site for it. It's to be called Point Douglas, I understand ".

"What's the origin of the name, Hugh?"

" It's one of Lord Selkirk's family names. Beyond that, don't ask me!"

Heney pulled a long stemmed pipe towards himself and offer   ed another to Peter who shook his head.

"Lot's of vices, but never that one, Hugh!"

"Some of Macdonell's men are making hay, clearing land and planting

Landing of the Selkirk Settlers. Red River, 1812

winter wheat, and another group is building another house called Fort Daer. Before you ask, I think it's another Selkirk family name!" Said Heney in between puffs at the pipe.

"It's to Fort Daer that I think I'll go, then" said Peter.

"I understood that you'd been given command of Brandon House Peter. That's a hell of a long way from Fort Daer. "

"That's right. John McKay moved on to Qu'Appelle House. I've left my son Thomas in charge in my place. He should be able to manage until I return".

Winter showed all its teeth.

160

The temperature slumped many degrees below that ever encountered by the newcomers. They were incapable of feeding themselves in the hostile environment and food had to be provided for them. Starvation was only just around the corner.

Peter acquired food from every possible source and concentrated on the women and children. He used resources from the prairies, Qu'Appelle and Pembina.

Mary was heavily pregnant, but she continued to work better than any of the men.

"I have to return to Brandon House, soon" he said to her as they sat leaning on each other in their quarters. Her head rested on his and he rubbed her swollen stomach gently.

"Boy or girl?" he asked.

"Not care. Think girl. Carrying different from boy. If boy, you name. If girl, I call her Faith. We need plenty faith in this place"

He put his right arm around her shoulder.

"I must go now that I have been promoted to Master Trader. Among my employees are both our sons, Thomas and Charles. If the journey is too much, you can stay here for the winter.

I'll miss you, but it won't be for long"

She sat up and shook her head violently.

"Not stop. Go with you. I can go OK".

They left next morning. It was not snowing, but the sky was menacing. The river currents carried patches of sharp ice floes.

However, they completed the journey to Brandon House without incident.

Winter faded and turned to spring. The eighth child, Faith, born in October, died suddenly.

The Spring of 1813 turned to glorious summer, but another tragedy struck. His daughter Decussrogan fell ill, remained so for 24 days, then died.

Macdonnel called at Brandon House on his way from York Factory back to Red River. He was taken to a small stockyard where Peter was washing down a reluctant bull.

"Well, well, well! Indeed you are a man of many talents, Peter! A bull-washer too!"

Peter laughed, wiped his forehead with the back of a hand, hung his bucket on a large nail.

"Welcome, welcome Miles. Very pleased to see you again. Yes, I've been called some things similar to that, I expect!. Are you being taken care of? I'll change my boots and come indoors. Mary will look after you until I'm decent"

Mary had stepped from the doorway and was walking towards Hugh. He turned and shook her hand.

"I couldn't wish to be in better company, Mary" he said, smiling at her, and linking arms, they went back to the cabin.

She showed Hugh a gun-chest that Peter had begun packing with Indian and Eskimo Handiwork.

"It for his brother, Joseph, in England. " she said as Macdonell admired the quality and skill of the pieces.

"He's a lucky brother indeed to be receiving these lovely items" he said. "Incidentally, where did he get the bull?"

"Bull? Oh yes. From Northwesters at Fort La Souris. Lot of money. Also bought cow and cockerel. They for your settlement at Red River.".

Macdonell's face lit up with pleasure.

"Adam and Eve have borne a calf, so we have the beginnings of a small herd. Can't include the cockerel in that expression, but it will produce its own crop of offspring, I hope!"

Peter hopped in the door on one foot struggling with a slipper.

"I caught the tail end of that conversation, Miles so you know about the bull and heifer. I was pleased to get them, irrespective of cost".

Mary brought two mugs of rum for the men.

"It's only a few weeks since I visited Point Douglas" said Peter. "Surveyed some lots to be granted to settlers."

"Yes. So I heard. Just missed you when you took the results to York Factory."

"When is the third batch of settlers due, Miles?"

"Quite soon, I'm told, so I shall go back home, to Point Douglas, then come out again to York and arrange to pick them up."

He sipped at the drink.

"Douglas is turning into a neat village. The fort is still being built. I'm not very happy about the field crops, but gardens seem to be flourishing. We've had a few of the sheep worried by dogs.."

He gave a big sigh.

"The Kildonian settlers are very late. About a year, I should think. We

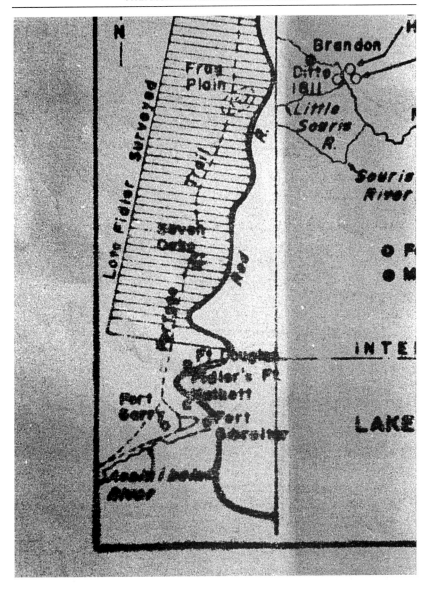

were expecting about 100 young men under Archibald McDonald, but no sign of 'em yet!".

"That was a tragedy, sure enough. I understand that plague broke out on the ship which was diverted to Churchill. They'll be expected to stay there for the winter, until the plague has gone, then to York and on to Red River by boat. "

"Poor people" said Mary sadly.

"Yes. Poor people, right enough. I hope they are strong enough to survive the winter and fever together" said Peter, flopping down at the table.

"I think they will get some considerable support from a group comprising Canadians and Metis who want to join them at Red River." said Miles. "They can show the newcomers the ropes as we nautical men term it!"

"I shall be visiting the settlement quite soon" said Peter. "I'll try and make sure that arrangements are made for their reception"

The Northwesters Organise

Simon McGillivray wrote to his partners in the North West Company about Selkirk's settlers:

*"It will require some time and I fear, cause much expense to us as well as to himself before he is driven to abandon the project, **yet he must be driven to abandon it,** for his success would strike at the very existence of our trade."*

"We've arrived at a critical time, Peter" welcomed Miles Macdonell. "That strutting fool at Fort Gibraltar has issued warrants for the arrest of me and my Sheriff John Spencer"

Peter was looking at the Fort through his telescope.

" Is that Duncan Cameron in the rather splendid uniform?"

Miles spluttered with anger.

"It's not even his uniform! It belongs to Major A N McLeod!

The Voyageur Corps has been disbanded, but they've made him an officer in it anyway!

There was a frantic knocking at the door, which burst open to admit two clerks.

"Sorry Mr Macdonnell! But they've got Mr Spencer and placed him under arrest." gulped one.

"And the colonists are arming themselves to set him free" panted the other.

"Thank you, men" said Macdonell, sitting down to pull on his black boots, "I shall be out shortly"

"Don't forget there's a warrant for you too" observed Peter.

"What exactly do you intend to do".

"I shall go across to Gibraltar and have it out with Cameron. You can remain here if you wish"

"Not likely!" said Peter, "Wouldn't miss this bit of excitement for the world."

They eased themselves through the crowd of angry settlers who were brandishing pick-handles, staves, an occasional gun.

"What yer gonna do Mr Macdonell?"

"Give 'em one in the eye for me!"

"I'd stick that uniform up his..." but the rest was droned by noise.

"I don't think you should go" said Peter at the jetty. "They've used the warrant to take Spencer. You'll be making it easier for them if you walk straight into their arms. They will have cut off the colony's head and arms at one attempt. No. I'll go and meet you here when I get back. Does that suit you?"

Macdonell eventually agreed with great reluctance.

On his return, Peter conveyed bad news to Macdonell.

"Sorry, Miles. Didn't take any notice of me. They are concerned about getting him away quickly, though. They've already put him in a canoe and transported him to the east, for trial they say"

"Not wasting any time, are they!" said Macdonell.

"No, they aren't, and not only that, I spoke to a couple of Metis when I was over there. They didn't want to be seen talking to me, which is unusual! But the Westers have appointed Cuthbert Grant as 'Captain of the Metis'"

"Grant? Grant? Isn't he the son of Grant the Assiniboine trader?"

"He is" said Peter. "And a very intelligent young man too, by all accounts. Another bit of bad news is that the Westers are going to offer rewards for colonists to desert. If that takes hold, it will be bad news for colonists and Red River too".

"Well. A nice pickle things seem to be in! I suppose we'll just have to be prepared and deal with things as they arise. Let's go and get a helping of your wife's Indian tea while we think about it"

Near Miss Again

Peter walked into the stock room where John was talking with two colonists. They all smiled at him and the two colonists left.

"Morning John. I got your message. What about 'Old Bonneau'?"

"I've been checking back on our heavier debtors" said John pointing to the stock book.

" 'Old Bonneau' is up to the eyeballs. I think it's about time that I went and reminded him."

Peter looked at the ledger, turned over s number of pages and whistled.

"Hadn't realised it was so much" he said. "Can he pay?"

"You'd have to be armed, I think. He's a cantankerous devil. Shoot as soon as speak. Anyway, I wanted you to be aware that he's over with the Northwesters."

"I'll take a stroll over there in about half an hour. See what turns up"

Back in his quarters, he checked a pistol, put it in his pocket, and swung a sword at his waist.

Walking towards the river, he met Bonneau and a Northwester approaching.

"I've come to have a few words with you, Mr Bonneau" said Peter as they drew near.

They were about 24 feet apart. Bonneau dived to the side of the track, raised his shotgun and fired at Fidler.

The shot tore through Peter's jacket, cut away a pocket and struck the barrel of the pistol. The Northwester stood stock still.

Bonneau ran away towards a tent in the undergrowth about 100 yards away and reloaded.

Fidler followed him.

"Lay down the gun, Mr Bonneau and let's talk sensibly. I'm not injured, so everything's fine"

"Don't come any closer, Fidler. I don't trust yer. Come closer and I'll blow yer head off!"

Peter stood still and made no move. Then, slowly, he turned, showing his back, and walked the way he had come.

Back at the trading post, he sent some men to collect Bonneau, which they did without a struggle.

Later, Cameron came over from Fort Gibraltar to ask for his release and Fidler let him go.

Peter went back to take charge of Brandon House for the winter of 1814 - 1815 and on 24th November, his son Clement was born. Mary and he were now the proud parents of eight living children.

In his absence, things appeared to go from bad to worse at the settlement. Mary was quite distressed at events.

"I am afraid for all our people" she said "Cuthbert Grant is becoming very swollen-headed"

"I think Miles is helping Cuthbert's cause, Mary, whatever it is, by issuing proclamations which the Metis see as not being in their interests. The one outlawing buffalo hunting on horseback for example. It's the Metis who mostly hunt on horseback, the Indians and colonists on foot."

"That is so, Peter, but did you know that Miles had arrested Bostonais Pangman for buffalo- hunting by horse?"

"No! I haven't heard that. What else do they say?"

"Well, they say Cuthbert imprisoned some of Miles' men. Nothing serious happened, though. It very good story for Northwesters to spread among Metis. It joins all Metis to hate settlers and Hudson's Bay people".

"It reminds me of when I set fire to the forest!. These things can get out of control so you have to take great care to check them. We are due to return there in May, so I hope everything has quietened down by then".

It was 19th May that Fidler returned. The atmosphere had changed for the worse and seemed taut as a fiddle string.

Macdonell had lost weight, he carried a haunted look, but his voice was strong.

His room was warm and well lit.

"The Westers are turning the screws on us Peter." he said angrily. "The woods are full of Metis under the control of Cuthbert Grant. He's brought a gang of them from Edmonton, or at least, the Westers have. I've had to start teaching army manoeuvres to the colonists!"

"What's this about guns, Miles?"

"Oh God! Don't mention guns to me! Last week, I took a group to the prairie edge to see what the buffalo situation is. When we got back, the Westers had dismantled the artillery and taken it to Fort Gibraltar!

"What did you do?"

"Not a lot to do. I arrested some of the Metis who were alleged to have helped, but Grant kidnapped some of my men. I had to swap them."

"If it wasn't so serious, it could almost be funny " said Peter.

"It's not funny since this morning, I can tell you. Some settlers' horses have been killed. All by arrows. The Northwesters and Metis reckon the Indians did it"

"It's certainly out of character for the Indians to do it. Steal them, yes! Kill them, no!"

"Then, there's George Campbell. " slumping back into the buffalo lined chair. "He's a lazy no-good that I've had lots of trouble with. He deserted to Cameron and persuaded some other colonists to go with him. They've all gone to Ontario, I'm told"

Miles filled a pipe with tobacco, stamped it into the bowl with a carved buffalo bone.

"As if that wasn't enough, Peter, Elizabeth McKay has gone to live with Grant."

Peter was surprised.

"Elizabeth! John McKay's daughter?"

Macdonell nodded miserably.

"Oh no!. I've counted John as one of my friends since Hudson's Bay. It's not so much Cuthbert Grant, but the times we are in." Said Peter.

On 29th May, Peter was called to the watchtower.

" John Rowand arrived from Fort Edmonton with more Metis and canoes." said Miles, pointing . "Grant has mustered his army where they can blockade exits and entries from and to the settlement."

On June 5th thirteen Hudson's servants left and went quite openly to the Northwesters.

Two days later, a message came that Westers were to attack the trading post. Miles and Peter organised their men to keep watch in shifts 24 hours a day.

The attack didn't materialise but that same afternoon 25 mounted men who crossed Frog Plain to join the Metis came across Hudson's Bay cattle. They killed the largest bull and rustled the rest.

Forty two settlers had become disenchanted with the tough way of life and anti-social neighbours. They chose to join the Northwesters and were despatched out of the area. by canoe

Fidler and Macdonell inspected the lookout points that night.

"We'll do it in shifts, Mac, and keep the staff in shifts too, with arms." said Peter.

A missile smacked into the pallisade near Peter's head and he ducked as the rifle barked.

Macdonell was a fraction behind him as a second missile struck and whined off into the darkness.

They crouched and made their way around the fortifications.

Ahead of them, McLeod and others bobbed up and down, firing at the enemy gun flashes.

McLeod howled suddenly and his gun flew over the parapet.

He gripped his wrist and hopped around, shouting with pain.

A ball had shattered McLeod's hand.

Within seconds of treating McLeod and helping him down the ladder, Mr Warren was struck by a fragment which left a hole in his skull an inch and a quarter in diameter. It was thought that he was dead, but he showed signs of life, even though some of his brains leaked through the hole. He wasn't expected to live.

Eventually, the sniping ceased. Men sat down until their relief arrived. The message about Mr Warren's condition was passed around to glum, serious faces.

Mr McLeod was expected to lose the use of his hand, probably have it amputated.

The settlement Councillors met on 17th June at Mr Warren's cabin to discuss recent events. They were Miles Macdonell, Peter Fidler, Doctor James White, Archibald McDonald and James Sutherland.

"The steps we've taken so far have been the only ones to take, I believe" said James White.

"It's a good thing that we tore down the old block house. That's been the main cover for our attackers" Sutherland added.

"It hasn't been much help since they tore down that section of the palisade and erected the damn canon there! I'm looking right at it! It's pointing this way!" said Macdonell, stepping away from the window opening.

"We've now lost all the horses since the Metis rounded them up two days ago" added Fidler, quietly. "I've been tempted to go out and pull down their damn flag, and kick over that 5 gallon keg of rum! We've lost 13 men to them what with fear and love of rum!"

"And that was by eight o'clock yesterday morning when they had only just put the stuff out". Said Sutherland scathingly.

"I've been thinking things over" said Macdonell. "A lot of this is because they have a warrant out for my arrest. I think the situation might cool if I surrender myself to them."

As the others protested, he threw up his hands.

"No, no, no! I've decided and that's what I shall do. They'll probably send me out to the east for trial. I don't expect them to murder me in cold blood!"

He looked around .

"In my absence, of course, Peter will be in charge. I wish you all good luck. Don't worry. It will work out OK".

He shook hands with everyone, changed his clothes and walked alone to the Northwesters camp. They arrested him gleefully and led him away.

Next day, Peter went to Fort Gibraltar to effect a release for Miles and to make some sort of peace with them.

"Nothing to do with us! " they said. "It's the Metis you need to treaty with" Peter met Grant.

"The settlement must go. These people are not wanted here. "

As Grant spoke, the smoke and flames from several house fires could be seen. One was McLean's house.

Chief Peguis with 33 braves of the Bungees had joined Peter to talk with the leader of the Metis. He attempted to mediate, but Grant would have none of it.

He pulled a rolled document from his pocket urged his horse forwards and thrust the document into Fidler's hand.

"Come tomorrow to this place with an answer" he said, waved his arm and the Metis swung around and left. Peter read the ultimatum back in the trading house, surrounded by the other Councillors.

"1. All settlers to retire immediately from this river, no appearance of a colony to remain.

2. Peace and amity to subsist between all parties, traders, Indians and freemen, in future, throughout these two rivers and on no account any person to be molested in his lawful pursuit

.3. The honourable Hudson's Bay Company will, as customary, enter this river with, if they think proper, from three to four of their former trading boats and from four to five men per boat as usual.

4. Whatever former disturbance has taken place between both parties, that is to say, the honourable Hudson's Bay Company and the Half-breed of the Indian territory, to be totally forgot and not to be recalled by either party.

5. Every person retiring peaceable from this river immediately shall not be molested in their passage out.

6. No person passing the summer for the Hudson's Bay Company shall remain in the buildings of the company but shall retire to some other spot, where they will establish for the purpose of trade..

Signed by Cuthbert Grant, Bostonais Pangman, William Shaw,

Bonhomme Montour (The Four Chiefs of the Half-Breeds)
  Red River Territory.25th June 1815.
  The Councillors could find no way out which would not lead to bloodshed.
  They capitulated.
  Fidler left on 27th June with everything that could be crammed into 6 boats, including cattle, sheep, goods.
  Yet again, Fidler's last view was of destruction as the victorious Metis charged backwards and forwards through the green crops.
  Smoke soared into the sky from the fired fort and buildings.
  As McGillivray had wanted : " they were driven to abandon it"

CHAPTER 11

More Wars With Northwesters & Metis

(1816-1821)

From 1809 to 1814 the Hudson's Bay Company paid no dividends.
In 1815 it paid only 4%.

But, the NorthWesters hadn't realised it would be so difficult to destroy their competitors.

The Hudson's Bay Company had a long history of ups and downs, had retained the 'will to win' and because most of the shareholders were wealthy businessmen with diverse interests, had the resources to bounce back to the top.

Wedderburn's management policy ensured that the Company stuck to its revised strategy. Tactics had been evolved and agreed and were

"York Factory" Samuel Hearne

(Provincial Archives P228)

172

implemented by its commanders in the field.

Slowly but surely the company climbed back to its previous position.

Colin Robertson, an ex-Northwester, was to be the principal tool for rejuvenation and he was determined to fight fire with fire.

Despatched by Wedderburn and the committee to exercise the new tactics within the framework of established policy, he was intent on re-establishing the Athabascan post at Red River.

As Miles Macdonell, under arrest, with 140 ex-colonist prisoners, canoed along the Red River, Robertson passed them,

travelling in the opposite direction with 16 canoes of volunteers that he had recruited from Montreal, the home-base of the Northwesters!

His motto was ' When among wolves, howl!'

An able man, good leader, very extrovert, he despatched a force of men to re-occupy Red River colony. He turned back and on Lake Winnipeg to meet Peter Fidler with Bird and Thomas.

"Bloody Hell" breathed Bird. "Will you take a look at this, Peter!"

Fidler leaned forward, took the telescope and trained it along the river where Bird was pointing.

A fleet of boats and canoes filled the waterway. The first one flew Hudson's Bay flag.

One of the newcomers fired three shots into the air, presumably to attract their attention, but one group could hardly miss the other.

"Keep in close, Mr Thomas" shouted Peter " in case it's a trick. Stand by your arms men".

The new boats swept alongside them. A tall, red-headed man shouted across

"Fidler? I'm Colin Robertson. Come to pick you up and go to Red River colony. "

"Go alongside him, please " said Peter and his canoe moved easily through the water in a few strokes.

"Pleased to meet you Colin" said Peter. "Don't think I'll risk a hand-shake!. We were on our way to Norway House on the Jack River"

"I understand you are, Peter, but I've countermanded that instruction. It's to Red River we'll go and show 'em we mean business this time".

He waved his hand to encompass his force.

"There are 157 Canadians and 20 officers here. With your men, we shall need some stopping"

Peter's group joined him.

Robertson took command of Fidler's settlers and returned to the colony.

Fidler and several others sat around a blazing fire to listen to Robertson

"I don't know whether you are aware of it, but the Company has paid no dividends between 1809 and 1814. In 1815, it did, but only 4%. The businessmen among you will realise that large amounts of money are being lost by the investors. They want it to stop and Mr Wedderburn's strategy is designed to do just that."

He looked around at the intent faces. All were interested.

"It will not be fast, but we shall climb back to our previous leading position. I know from personal experience that the North West Company didn't realise how difficult it would be to destroy us. We have the will to win and we shall bounce back again."

"He looked round once more.

"You may be aware by now that my group passed Miles Macdonell under arrest and 140 ex-colonists before we met Mr Fidler's group. I couldn't stop for a number of reasons, one of which was that my 16 canoes were full of volunteers recruited from Montreal, the North Wester's home base!. "

He smiled at the group.

"But that will change. I shan't pass any more. My motto is 'when among wolves, howl!' Tomorrow, we shall dig in, and the following day, we shall re-occupy Red River Colony"

Two days later they re-entered the colony.

McLeod's Blacksmith's shop still stood.

With his four men, McLeod had fought off the Metis and Northwesters alike.

Crops which had survived were nearly ready for gathering, buffalo were in great numbers nearby and there were fish in the river.

"Peter, " said Robertson as they landed, "Be so kind as to set the men to harvesting and food gathering for the winter"

It was an activity which the settlers and soldiers alike performed with great pleasure.

Robertson gave the impression that he knew what he was doing and his talents spread beyond his management of the colonists.

He could manage the Metis, too.

His strutting extroversion won their admiration and friendship so that they were pleased to sell provisions to him.

The second evening, he talked long and confidentially with Peter who was was suddenly in great demand at several places.

"Peter, Thomas Thomas, the Governor of the Northern department, has selected you for another task. He wanted improvements made along the waterway at York and its contacts inland.

He believes that you are the man to do it and wants me to send you to discuss it with him in York.". He nibbled at a hard, sweet biscuit.

"Oxford Lake Post, for example, built some years ago by William Sinclair is now proving inadequate.

It means of course that you will be obliged to move some considerable distance downstream to Knee Lake to build Knee Lake House to replace Oxford. What do you feel about it?".

Peter was silent for a while, then said " It is a project I have thought about. It should be designed as a half-way house and I expect that it will take several men three years to complete. It would be a summer retreat for a couple of weeks for traders. Trade goods would be sent from York to Knee Lake and the traders would collect them, then go about their business."

"Mr Thomas knew what he was talking about Peter. I'll leave you to organise it, then"

On his way, Fidler met D Sutherland commanding four boats laden with colonists and goods, the latest batch of settlers from Scotland.

Fidler spent less than a month getting new buildings laid out at Knee Lake and left them to continue on 22nd August whilst he visited York.

Three days later, he arrived at his destination at the same time as new group of settlers arrived from Britain.

Their ship had anchored on 26th August, carrying 84 colonists, but was travelling with a cargo of sawn wood down the Bay to Moose Factory.

The Company, as part of its policy of diversification abroad, went into the lumber business. Furs remained the first priority, but timber from the Red River settlement was seen as an important secondary consideration.

A proposed new interest was mining. A mineralogist from England, Mr John Rogers, arrived with the English group and discussed Peter's early reports.

The Governor of all the Hudson's Bay territories, known as "Rupert's

175

Land", Mr Robert Semple, together with Mr William Sinclair, who had been on leave for a year, arrived together on August 28th 1815 as passengers.

The arrival of Semple meant that the hierarchical structure from top to bottom was Semple, Robertson, Macdonell. whilst Thomas Thomas was appointed Governor of the north.

William Auld's resistance to settlement on the Red River was tantamount to a rejection of his Company's policy, and he was called home and fired..

Sinclair became a Councillor of Semple's and was instated by Thomas Thomas as the Master of Knee House, which Fidler was building.

Robertson was left to pick up the pieces from the Red River area and was given a lieutenant, Alexander Macdonell, a cousin to the Northwester ' Whitehead' Macdonell of the same name.

Then Fidler was given the job of transporting Semple and the Red River colonists to their destination.

Fidler recorded in his journal that Macdonell and the first two boats, leaving on 6th September, took more of their own gear than Company goods!.

"I've gotta have a word with you, Mr Fidler" said the steersman

"Certainly Mr Flett. Go ahead"

"In all my life, I've never had to take pigs. Pigs! I arst you. Pigs! It's a long way and we'll have to portage in some places, but I ain't carryin' pigs. Nosir! No pigs."

"Um, yes. I, ah, hear what you say Mr Flett. Is that your last word?"

"I'm sorry Mr Fidler, but 'tis. No pigs!"

"Right Mr Flett. That's not exactly a problem. It means rescheduling pigs elsewhere. Now. I've got a canon that needs conveying. It's almost as heavy as the pigs but it doesn't grunt, make a mess, want feeding. Nevertheless, it does want carrying at portage. What do you feel about that?"

"Don't sound too bad, Mr Fidler. What weight we talkin' about?

"I think it'll be two 3 pounders Mr Flett to replace those stolen by the Northwesters"

"In that case, consider it a good swap, Mr Fidler and here's my hand on it".

On the 9th, Peter had words with his sone, Charles.

"Charles, will you be the steersman-in-charge of tomorrows boats. There will be two of them. One with colonists but the other with their property?"

"Of course, Dad. " said Charles, shortly, with a pleased smile.

So the further two boats were sent on their way on 10th September;

Charles led the first group as the steersman, allocated to Brandon House. Subsequent reports record that Charles was sober, honest and industrious.

The boat of goods went to Jack River house to supply the Montreal 'voyageurs'.

On the 15th September, Peter called together the leaders of each of the final four boats

"This should be the last leg to the settlement, gentlemen. You are not all experienced at this kind of travel, but don't worry. We'll try to stop long enough for you to regain your wind. I don't pretend that it is easy, but I promise that we'll make it together."

He looked around.

"It is not uncommon for boats or canoes to capsize. If you do, try not to panic. You are our first priority. Of course, if I capsize, I want to be your first priority"

They laughed and the nervousness disappeared.

On 16th September. Fidler accompanied a final group of four boats.

As predicted, one capsized. Occupants were saved, but goods went to the bottom of the river..

On 10th October, Peter came across Charles and a boat.

"What's the problem, son?" he called as they closed.

Charles pointed. A woman was obviously in the last stages of labour.

"Mr Macdonell told me to wait until the baby was born" he said apologetically.

Peter waited and then travelled along with them.

As they approached Jack River colony, a boat appeared.

"Ahoy there, Hudson's Bay. Pembrum from Jack River. "

They drew alongside and greeted him.

"Some food for you all. Salted catfish and potatoes"

"What's the food situation like, Mr Pembrum" asked Peter.

"Well, we've produced 400 bushels of wheat, 300 bushels of barley and plenty of potatoes. Meat is plentiful as buffalo are swarming in hundreds at Fort Daer".

A schooner, with other boats, took colonists south along Lake Winnipeg.

It was whilst on this journey that Colin Robertson's progress was reported to Fidler.

"You can't believe what's agoin' on there, Peter.

Robertson has made it up with the Metis. He's even persuaded 'em that they were tools of the Westers!. Grant is saying he's sorry for what he's done. Can ya' believe it!"

"What about the settlers, though?" asked Peter.   .

"He's keeping the settlers occupied. But the Metis, he's planted the seeds of doubt in their minds and they began to realise that they had been used as pawns in the Northwesters' game!".

Pembrun chuckled and slapped Peter on the back.

"But wait till I tell you the next bit. You'll never believe this one! Robertson waited until he could catch Duncan Cameron off-guard and then arrested him!. Then, he up with his soldiers and occupied Fort Gibraltar!"

Pembrun spat into the river..

"And that ain't the last of it. No sirree. He persuaded Cameron to make promises of future good behaviour towards the Hudson's Bay settlement, and then turned Fort Gibraltar back to him. Can you believe it? This is fighting fire with goddammed fire and the Northwesters don't know which way to jump!"

Lord Selkirk was due to visit Montreal and so Roberstson selected the ablest man from his group of voyageurs, to take letters and a report progress to him.

Jean Baptiste Lagimodiere was the messenger. It was his wife from Quebec who had been the first white woman to have a child in the North west in 1808.

Lagimodiere's trip with one companion, is a story in its own right. An epic journey lasting from late October for 1800 miles through the Northwest Company's heartland. He proceeded on foot through the middle of winter and arrived at Montreal on 10th March.

Fidler and his party, in the meantime, were delayed by ice on Lake Winnipeg, so Governor Semple with Fidler and Sutherland hurried on ahead and walked into the colony on 3rd November.

It was a few days later that Peter was able to report progress to Governor Semple.

"I've set the new settlers some tasks. Half of them are threshing corn, even during the night, whilst the other half I've sent off under supervision to rebuild the Capel House trading post."

"Well done, Peter. I thought the Capel House post was still standing?"

"No, Governor. It was burned down by the Northwesters. Incidentally, I must say that the newcomers were very pleased, and surprised, as was I, to find crops of wheat and barley, here."

"I noticed that a lot of the old people, squaws and children were moving away this morning. I meant to enquire the reason but haven't had time until now. Do you know why?"

"Indeed I do, Governor. 'Whitehead' Macdonell, the Northwesters' Master, threatened to shoot all Hudson's Bay men if they were still around in 24 hours.

But this time, the local Indians have taken a hand in the game and sided with us. They send their old people, squaws and children away when preparing for battle."

"So what has Macdonell done?"

"I'm pleased to say that he recognised the danger signals and backed down, allowing my men to continue their building."

Semple, having sized up the situation said "I've decided to send the settlers on to Pembina, to Fort Daer, a place where buffalo is plentiful. I know they won't be very happy at the idea of moving so I'm going to send you to be Master at Brandon House. That should encourage them."

"Can't say I'm over-the-moon myself, Governor. Mary's only just unpacked and it means that my family has another 8 days' journey to their new quarters. A journey on foot of about sixty miles! No, she definitely won't be happy".

From his new trading post, along the Assiniboine, Peter kept an ear cocked to happenings at the settlement and recorded news in his journal.

His own unpleasant experiences at Red River may have left him with a wariness about its likely success.

He was employed doing what he did best, communicating with the Indians, trading with the prairie Indians. He understood their way of life and was sympathetic when they had trouble.

John McLeod the Blacksmith who had remained behind when Red River settlement was burned down, took a prominent part in showing the settlers how to hunt buffalo.

He rode into Fidler's post with three settlers.

When they were settled and given a tankard of rum each, John told of their recent harrowing experiences.

"We stayed at a Bungee encampment about fifteen miles from Turtle River. When evening came, we left to set up our own camp some eight miles away.

During the night, Sioux made a surprise attack on the Bungees and from a small band of thirty four, they'd murdered thirty one.!"

John swallowed heavily. One of the colonists rushed outside, retching. The others were very quiet and pale.

"It was me who discovered the bodies of the Bungees a coupla' days later. They'd all been killed and scalped except for a couple of women".

The youngest colonist said in a strained voice.

"I'll never forget it! Most of 'em had been half roasted. Several had arms and legs cut off. Some still had knives sticking in their throats."

He became silent, his eyes filled with remembered horror.

John placed an arm round him and patted his back like a father.

Peter nodded, understandingly.

"It's only been two years ago since a similar massacre had happened when Sioux killed a party of Bungees . Four months before that they slaughtered a group of French Canadians hunting buffalo".

"I try to keep my people's mind off such matters if I can. I keep them fairly close to the fort, but can't always manage it. When they go out, it's with arms and enough men to defend themselves"

He stood, walked to the doorway and pulled aside the heavy buffalo-skin curtain.

"I'm sure you will have noticed that the men have been put to work making kegs, repairing weapons, and many other tasks. They are repetitive, John, but important and keep everyone busy"

He walked back into the large room. The curtain fell silently. .

" I've been watching Mr Smith and one man making nails. I didn't realise before how it was done!. They split a bar then chop and shape pieces. It's very time consuming and I reckon it would be cheaper and much less arduous to buy the nails already made. Innovation. One of the joys of being Master!"

"Don't forget that I'm a Blacksmith, Peter! If your ideas spread, I'll be out of a job!"

Even the two colonists smiled."

"You have two of your sons working for you now, I understand" said John, easing himself on the heavy wooden chair.

Peter beamed.

"Yes. I have. They've certainly sprung up. Thomas is now aged twenty and Charles is seventeen. I try to make sure they learn all the crafts there are to be learned at the post. Thomas is employed as a Writer. He's good with figures and calculations so I've tried to make sure that he also learns a great deal about Astronomy."

A woman came in with a bark tray. It contained the makings for Indian tea.

"Well Brandon House certainly looks as though it's prospering" said John.

." Certainly meat is plentiful. I sent Thomas and Charles with dogs and sleds to procure meat a short while ago. They returned with 1,337 pounds !" His smile showed his pride at the feat.

"How do you arm your hunters, Peter?"

"Well, I normally allow a hunter four balls and four loads of powder. If they use three balls accurately, then they can keep the remainder. If they perform poorly, they had to pay for the extra balls and powder."

He poured boiling water over the tea leaves.

"Buffalo are everywhere. On 8th February I recorded that there were about 200 buffalo not more than two miles away.

A traveller from the Red River settlement reported having to force his way through a herd of cow buffalo within eighteen miles of the fort.".

"The Red River settlers still expect you to supply them with meat, fat and pemmican. A goddam annoyance when they have food in plenty on the doorstep. Those at Fort Douglas should be told to go out and get their own!" .Peter nodded.

"I hate complaining, but I feel that in their own interests, that action should have been taken earlier whilst it was still spring.. Dogs and horses were on hand to help with the hunting and it would have been comparatively easy to lay in a good stock of meat for when the snow and ice cleared."

A loud voice shouted "Express!" It was the annual express from Edmonton. It had travelled via Hudson's House, Charlton House and Kapel, arriving at Brandon House .

181

"Excuse me while I open the mail, John. The rider will only be in the bunkhouse for a short while. If there's anything to send on with him I shall have to send it quickly".

He read the correspondence.

"That's good news. " He said out loud. Then to John.

"Colin Roberstson has decided to lead an expedition to compete with the Northwesters at Chipewyan even though there's no longer a Hudson's Bay fort there. It was destroyed, as you know"

John nodded. The third colonist came into the room still looking shaky. The others moved along on their bench to give him room.

"He's appointed John Clarke to build Fort Wedderburn on the Lake Athabasca site with outposts at Hay River, Great Slave Lake and Lesser Slave Lake."

"Isn't he another former Northwester?" said John, frowning.

"He is, John, and Clarke is to lead the expedition in place of Robertson".

Peter glanced down at the documents, turned one over and said

"He's also re-establishing the old posts at Green Lake and Isle-A-La-Crosse. I hope that it all works out for us".

"I've had a taste, like you, of what the Northwesters can do, Peter. They are stubborn and violent. I fear the worst, I reckon"

He looked at his three colleagues.

"I think a long rest is in order, Peter. If you'll fix us up, we'll make it a long nights sleep and leave early tomorrow."

As McLeod gloomily forecast, the determination of the Northwesters was so great and so violent that they cancelled out Clarke's attempts in the north.

Archibald McGillivray, at Fort Vermilion, was responsible for starving out one of Clarke's representatives George McDougald, who was eventually obliged to turn over his furs and goods to McGillivray.

The escape of his men is a story of tragedy.

Local Indians were savaged by Northwesters as they attempted to feed the sixteen starving Englishmen. The group trudged on foot over frozen Lake Athabasca, but individuals fell out, one by one, until only three survived.

The other thirteen died of starvation in a land of plenty.

Governor Semple and subsequently, Fidler, were both law-abiding citizens who found it difficult to comprehend the lengths to which the Northwesters would stoop to achieve their ends.

Fidler recorded his sadness at the disaster. No one knew better than he what the Northwesters could muster in that region.

He wrote that " greater numbers and a greater show of force would be imperative to get a foot hold."

Capturing the Northwester Fort
17th March

Someone waved a Hudson's Bay flag.

Among the trees on the other side, shots rang out.

Dozens of men ran towards Fort Gibraltar from all directions. The two palisade gates were open, Indians froze where they stood.

Canadians flung themselves to the ground. Robertson led the occupying forces and he shouted and yelped as did his men.

"Round the trading cabin, lads " he shouted, and rushed into another building where figures were coming to the door.

The Master, Cameron, without a jacket and wearing thick braces, stood red faced and open mouthed at the commotion and panic across the compound.

"What the bloody Hell is goin' on here?" He bawled above the uproar.

Some of the Canadians were lying on the ground, hands behind their neck.

"You are my prisoner, Cameron. One false move and I'll cut off your ears!"

Cameron looked angry but dazed.

"Robertson! You'll pay for this you low-life scum" he snarled, hitching up one sagging bracer.

"Two false moves and I sever that lang nose a'yourn" crowed Robertson. "Now get inside. Now! Now! Quickly!"

He pricked Cameron with the point of his claymore took Cameron prisoner and occupied the post.

A horse thundered into the compound. It's rider jumped off, secured the horse to the hitching rail, then looked around. He took in the scene incredulously then dived to get back on the horse but was prevented.

Robertson confiscated all the correspondence.

"Just in time for the express mail, I believe" said Robertson.

"Set up positions around the fort as planned, lieutenant. I shall be in my new quarters, that is, the ex-quarters of Mr Cameron"

One of the letters gave details of the Northwesters intention to organise the Metis aided by the half-breed Cuthbert Grant, during the spring and destroy the new colony. The letter was from Fort Vermilion to John Dugald Cameron at Saulte St.Marie.

One piece of information from Europe via Montreal indicated that Napoleon Bonaparte had been defeated and narrowly escaped capture

"I think that this should be communicated to Mr Semple, Mr Macdonell and Mr Fidler" said Robertson

Fidler quoted the whole of the letters into his records then discussed the situation with the local Indians.

He told them that on 26th March, Cuthbert Grant was to be made Captain General of the Metis and that the half breeds were assembling around the region so that about 150 would attack the colony and drive out Hudson's Bay settlers and traders

Lone Feather put one hand on Fidler's shoulder.

"Brother, we are divided on the matter. I am with you. Many others are with you. But it is your dispute with other white men. Some of my people are not sympathetic because they know how strong are the Northwesters."

"Thank you Lone Feather. I am pleased that you do not hide your opinions or feelings. I have always trusted you. However, I trust the Metis much less at the moment."

He hesitated.

"Will you act as go-between with my people and the Metis?

In the meantime, I shall ask Governor Semple for ten well-armed men just in case we are attacked by the Northwesters or anyone else".

Indians and Metis alike were stealing horses, and so, in April. Fidler sent every horse he had to help plough the land at Red River.

Robertson's continuing tactics were hurting the Northwesters.

He blockaded the Red River near Fort Douglas and prevented them passing with much needed food and supplies.

So the Northwesters reversed roles.

When James Sutherland brought a load of pemmican down river, they were held-up at gunpoint by about 60 mounted Metis.

The meat was stolen and added to a fleet of the Northwesters' boats about to descend Red River past Fort Douglas and its canons.

Cuthbert Grant's Metis split into two groups, one either side of the river, to guard the fleet.

Fidler received the information and instructed John Lyons to take the news, but Lyons became sick overnight. Alternatively, Thomas Favel refused to go. The only trustworthy person left was his son Charles who took a friend with him, only to be apprehended by the Metis, disarmed and sent back.

By 1st June, the pemmican armada was close to Fidler's Brandon House.

Whitehead Macdonald was with the fleet and he set off for the Northwesters Fort nearby with an escort of about 48 Metis, Canadians, Freemen and Indians on horseback, beating drums, singing Indian songs and waving a blue flag described as being four feet square and a figure of eight horizontally in the middle.

Fidler's men watched the proceedings from the fort parapet.

Appearing to be riding towards the Northwesters fort, the group turned suddenly and as one man rushed into the Hudson's Bay yard.

They tied up their horses, raised a flag above Hudson's and nailed one to the door.

Cuthbert Grant entered Fidler's quarters.

"Give me all the Fort keys, Fidler"

"Never, Cuthbert" said Fidler, grim and white faced.

Outside, the crowd then rushed to the warehouse, broke down the door and stole everything in it.

In spite, they tore up the cellar floor and cut out the parchment windows.

All the men carried gun sacks, a pike each and bows and arrows.

The small army stayed at Brandon House for only a short time, then, on 7th June, moved out, with 28 accompanying Grant on one bank and 10 with Antoine Hoole on the other.

Fidler began repair the Fort but moved out with his men to live with the Indians.

Even during this period, he collected four canoe-loads of furs and turned them over to Fort Norway.

Robertson and Semple fell out.

Robertson, the man of action, hearing about the attack on Fort Douglas, demanded that a force be organised immediately to ambush the Northwesters whilst they still had time.

He also proposed dismantling their Fort Gibraltar and using the timbers to reinforce Fort Douglas.

Semple prevaricated and nothing was done at that time.

Robertson refused to be involved with anything concerned with the region when all his advice was rejected and on 11th June set off for York Factor headquarters

The day after Robertson's departure, Semple had the fort dismantled.

Grant and the Metis decided to transport the precious pemmican overland past Fort Douglas' guns.

Semple, in the meantime, organised twenty five volunteers to confront them head on.

The two small armies met at Seven Oaks.

The Northwest contingent drew away from both groups so as not to be involved.

An Indian rode towards Semple's force .

"Keep back, all of you " called Semple . The Indian continued advancing, waving his weapons despite being told yet again to return.

One of Semple's men shot him.

There was a brisk fusillade of gunfire from both sides.

Grant shot Semple through the head and twenty of the Governor's force were dead.

Only one Indian was dead and one Metis from the opposing force.

Grant approached Fort Douglas and demanded its surrender. The occupants capitulated.

Having insisted on its complete abandonment, he guarded the inhabitants on their way down the Red River.

After almost one year, Selkirk's settlement had again come to ruin.

CHAPTER 12

Defeat of the Northwesters

(1816-1822)

J.B. Bird was appointed as Temporary Governor.

Robertson, accompanied by Fidler, made a report to the Governor In York on 12th August .

All were shocked by the outcome of the Seven Oaks confrontation, even though they had expected something like it. Robertson had shepherded the survivors of the battle and led them to Jack River Fort before meeting Fidler.

They met Miles Macdonell who was preparing to rendezvous with Lord Selkirk.

"He has recruited a small army of about a hundred   men" said Macdonell. "He's on his way westward to the colony and I'm to catch up

and go ahead".

He adjusted the saddle of his horse.

"I'm not sure that he knows abut the Seven Oaks disaster, but he'll find out soon enough. Then the sparks will fly! "

Selkirk was furious.

He slammed his fist into the canvas tent.

"Two can play this game! " he snarled. "We'll show them, Macdonell! Fort William shall be our revenge. Muster the men and make sure they are prepared for an attack"

They marched openly and captured Fort William with hardly any opposition.

Macdonell and two men brought out a struggling figure.

"Thought you might want to have words with this big fish, My Lord" Laughed Macdonell.

"Mr William McGillivray, by all that's holy! " said Selkirk gleefully."You are my prisoner, sir. "

"You'll pay dearly for this, Selkirk" spluttered McGillivray, Head of the Northwesters.

Selkirk turned and walked away, calling over his shoulder to Macdonell "Make him comfortable Mr Macdonell then report to me if you please"

"I'm planning to return to the Red River area, Mr Macdonell and take back what is rightfully the colonists property. I would wish for you and Captain D'Orsonnens of the brigade to attack and recapture Fort Daer. It may take until December to achieve that objective, but I want its name reverted to the original title, Fort Pembina"

He looked at Macdonell standing relaxed at the end of the wooden table.

"Do you foresee any difficulties?"

"Nossir. It shall be done"

"Very well. Similarly I would like your men to do the same with Fort Douglas in the New Year. Does that sound feasible?"

"Indeed it does, sir. I don't anticipate any serious problems"

And by January 10th 1817, Macdonell's men had indeed recaptured Forts Pembina and Douglas.

Peter Fidler sat by his wife's bed. She was in labour and he held her hand gently.

Two Indian midwives sat silently in the shadows by the fireplace.

"Tell me what's happening, husband" said Mary as a contraction passed through her.

"Yes dearest. If I begin to tire you, then tell me and I'll be quiet. "

She squeezed his hand understandingly.

"Well, first of all, I've sent messages to the 150 colonists still at Jack River, telling them what I know about Lord Selkirk's progress. I'm informed that the tougher ones have already set out over the ice of Lake Winnipeg and should be in their colony by early Spring."

His grip tightened against hers as a stronger contraction occurred.

"Unfortunately, I shall have to travel between Halkett Fort and Norway House as Jack River is to be called, to assist the settlers. Of course, I do expect to be here when our baby is born. Incidentally, sweetheart, if it is a girl, can we call her Colette. I can't think of a boy's name at the moment.!"

Her breathing had become more rapid and the midwives rose to their feet but stood motionless, attuned to Mary's condition.

"I am sending John Clarke to Fort Chipewyan. It is a difficult assignment, and he must pass through the Northwester's territory. He is aware of the dangers, of course and should take every precaution"

The midwives moved towards him quietly. He leaned and kissed Mary whose brow was beaded with sweat.

"I shall be in the next room if you want me, darling" he said in a choked voice and left.

Colette was born and Peter travelled to Norway House, where he met Governor Bird fresh from Edmonton House.

"There is nothing but bad news, Peter" said Bird, rocking from foot to foot in front of a roaring fire. "Disaster has followed disaster. Everything seemed to be going well and then it fell to pieces!"

Without waiting for comment, he went on

"John Clarke was attacked by the Northwesters and imprisoned at Fort Vermilion, I suppose you know?"

Peter nodded.

"I was told this morning" he said gravely.

"Well, all the Houses at Green Lake, Isle-A-La-Crosse, Lesser Slave Lake, Athabasca Lake and Pierre au Calumet have been robbed and the inhabitants taken prisoner"

"Can anything be done" asked Peter.

Bird shook his head. Blew upon his fingers.

"Because Clarke and others are held hostage, it is impossible for us to attack the Northwesters. But as a gesture of defiance, I have sent Decoigne to hold the Old Fort at Lake Athabasca where most of the fishing takes place"

"It's almost a year since the battle at Seven Oaks" said Peter thoughtfully " and its time for the Northwesters to ship their pemmican. Can anything be done about that?"

Bird considered the suggestion. Both sipped at their glass of wine.

"It's very dodgy indeed, Peter. Miles Macdonell and Cuthbert Grant will undoubtedly face one another and fight to the bitter end. I hope that Selkirk will arrive at Fort Douglas in time to provide a face-saving solution for both sides"

"I trust that the newly appointed Commissioner from Canada will arrive this year . Mr W B Colman whose principal brief is to maintain peace between our rival factions. He could spend a lot of time digging up the past, but whenever possible I think that he should persuade antagonists to let bygones be bygones.

"Well, I'm nearly fifty years of age now and have spent all my working life here" said Peter. "There is indeed much to be told to the Commissioner on both sides, but I doubt whether sufficient information can be gathered against one side or the other, anyway"

"I'm convinced you are right, Peter, and pray that things will be resolved speedily, without further aggravation. The Commissioner will be wise to call on people like yourself, wise in local ways, loyal and dependable."

He smiled, held out a hand and said goodbye.

Ownership Surrendered

Elegant as ever, Lord Selkirk sat up straight in the hard-backed chair smoking a long-handled Bolsover clay pipe.

"A pleasant, cool, smoke, Peter. I must confess not having heard of these pipes before"

"Not a habit I've ever acquired, My Lord. But I don't scorn it for a variety of reasons. One being that the pipes are made in my hometown in England. The other that they are used for ceremonials by the tribes. I imagine that you will be using them a lot more when you go ahead with your plan!"

Selkirk laughed. "Quite right. I hope to make a treaty with Chief Peguis and three other Chiefs on 18th July. I hope that they are agreeable to surrendering ownership of land along the Red River and other connected river-paths two miles in width."

"I imagine that the width will be greater at Forts Daer, Douglas and Grand Forks" said Peter thoughtfully.

"Exactly! That's the Surveyor speaking, Peter!. It will be closer to six miles, I believe"!

"I am grateful to you for inviting me to what must be a significant, historic event. I hope to make a copy of the document and identify the animals used by the Chiefs as their marks."

"I want more than that, Peter. I want you to survey strips of land for the settlers. I have enlisted the De Meuron Regiment into my brigade and they will be settling down on the east side of the Red River and building houses."

"What are the Chiefs getting in exchange for their land?"

"The Company has not been ungenerous. They will pay an annual 'quit' rent to the chiefs and warriors of the Chippeway or Saultaux Nation consisting of one hundred pounds of good and merchantable tobacco and the same to the chiefs and warriors of the Killistino or Cree nation"

"I shall start by measuring out several lots of land 100 yards in front of the east side of the river" said Peter, thoughtfully. "I intend to make a map of the Seven Oaks battle area whilst I have the opportunity."

"A very sad affair" intoned Selkirk.

Peter nodded.

"If my memory serves me right, I should be able to lay out about 33 lots of land, 100 yards in front from the little river below, on the east side to the mouth of the river".

"I want each settler to have a piece of land, with access to waster and a stand of trees, not to be cut down" said Selkirk enthusiastically. He stood and walked the room energetically.

"I intend to conduct my colonists on a tour of the site and show where certain community buildings could be. A church and a school, for example. I calculate that there should be a settlement for about two hundred persons and sixty houses".

Selkirk stretched, then stamped his booted feet.

"I know that you are leaving for Brandon House shortly and so I will leave you to complete your preparations. Be careful Peter. The Metis are still angry."

At the door, he turned.

"I don't have to ask for your word, Peter, but I may not be here when you return. I am obliged to go to the east to answer various legal charges. I regret that my enemies hereabouts seem to be many and so I shall be going by way of the United States."

He smiled briefly, nodded to himself, turned on his heel and left. The door closed quietly.

When Selkirk had left, Peter committed the conversation to his records

Two months later, the colonists were warned that Cuthbert Grant, leader of the Metis, was approaching. They barricaded themselves and prepared to do battle.

Into the first clearing rode a number of horsemen, led by Peter Fidler. Beside him was Grant and behind were some of Grant's trusted Metis.

Colonists crowded around the group and gaped as horsemen dismounted and entered an empty cabin.

"Call everyone for a meeting" instructed Peter and people jostled to find standing room inside and at the doors and windows.

"As you all know, I have been to Brandon House. Unfortunately, almost everything has been destroyed, but such things can be put right. More importantly, Mr Cuthbert Grant here " he said, nodding towards Grant, "has placed himself under my protection to visit Commissioner Colman".

He turned to Grant.

"Have you anything to add, Cuthbert?"

"I have " replied Grant.

He cleared his throat, waited until the buzz of surprise had subsided, then continued.

"I wish to meet the Commissioner and talk about our differences. I respect and trust Mr Fidler, an honest man, a brave fur-trader and himself the father of a respectable Metis family. There will be no more trouble".

After the colonists had left, a table and chairs were brought into the single room and an oil-lamp lit.

"I don't know how safe you'll be here, Cuthbert "said Peter. "The quicker you leave to visit the Commissioner, the safer you'll be, I reckon"

Grant smiled wryly.

"And that's the truth, Peter. " he said. "What will you be adoin'?"

"There have been some changes already that I noticed on the way in. There will be others that I haven't seen. I'm curious to find out what they are. Anyway, I have to visit Jack River House which is intended to be a new staging house between York and Lake Winnipeg. I think they are going to change its name permanently to Norway House because some Norwegians are extending it. Then I'm scheduled to return to Brandon House round about the 15th September as fur-trader. I look forward to that"

"What's in the future, Peter? What do you want to do?"

Peter gazed into the fire for a long minute.

"I've thought of retiring to my mother's stone house that I built for her five years ago. I've saved my salary, Cuthbert and always been careful. But I couldn't really go back."

He sighed.

"I could take Mary and the children and they'd live like lords, but I don't believe they would fit in very well. Everything is so different. No. I'll stay here. I love this country, anyway and with my family I shall retire and try to make them happy"

He looked towards a large chest in the corner.

"I want to organise my books"

He looked pointedly at Cuthbert then smiled.

"Including those taken over by you at Big Point House. Mr MacKay says you had some in your box, a bit muddied and torn, but still useable"

"I am truly sorry, Peter. But what was done, had to be done. Have I told you that some of the North West Company men have said that they will show you where they buried the canons from Fort Douglas?"

Peter whistled. "Now that's a turn-up for the books " he said with surprise. " They've been gone for a couple of years. I wonder if they still work? Anyway, that doesn't matter. The gesture does"

Three men appeared in the doorway. One pulled off his cap and said with agitation

"Mr Fidler, I've go some bad news about our bull"

"Come in lads, come in. Don't stand on too much ceremony. What's this about the bull?"

They looked from Peter to Cuthbert " It's all right, lads. You can speak in front of Mr Grant, Mr Myers. I have his parole. Now, what's happened to our one and only bull?"

From outside, a voice called

"It was me, Mr Fidler. It were a mistake."

"Who the Devil is that out there," said Peter. "Let him in"

193

A burly man holding a long rifle pushed his way into the cabin.

"Who are you , sir" asked Peter, eyeing him up and down.

"My name's Grant, Mr Fidler, Richard Grant. No relation" he said nodding towards Cuthbert. "Leastways, I don't think so"

"I works for the North West Company. 'Fraid I shot your bull. Accident, though. Thought it were a buffalo. 'Deed I did"

"A buffalo!. Not much like a buffalo Mr Grant. "

"And it were tethered, Mr Fidler" said Mr Myers angrily. "Had a large board over its forehead. On'y a fool ud think it were a buffalo" he looked as though he was about to spit but changed his mind.

"True though. " insisted Grant. "Did think it were a buffalo. Sorry .

"Is it dead, then?" asked Peter.

"No. Don't think so." replied Mr Myers. "It's still breathing, But it were a nasty wallop on its head."

Later, Peter wrote the incident into his records and noted "the bull has recovered and is now hauling wood"

"What were you doing at this post, Mr Grant"

"Well, I brought you a message Mr Fidler, from Mr Poitras of the North West Company. We don't have nobody who speaks the local Mandan lingo and you do. He suggests that you and him sends a joint group to the Mandans, pools their goods and splits the returns. The natives wants to deal with us, not with the Americans who are starting to travel up the Missouri River".

Peter thought about the suggestion. He could find no tricks or drawbacks, only improvements. He was aware of the continuing tribal battles between Sioux, Chippewas, Assiniboines , who had ceased to deal with traders or colonists.

"I shall let you know tomorrow, Mr Grant. Make yourself comfortable overnight and I'll give you my reply early. Mr Myers will look after you."

Grant left with a surly Myers who muttered

"I think damned buffalo!"

Cuthbert sat for dinner in Peter's cabin, surrounded by children. Peter nursed the new baby and occasionally tried to feed it with a spoon.

"I've had a look at some of your books, Peter" said Cuthbert, carving at a large steak. "Don't know where you get the space in your head to keep it all! But I'd like to go to school and get myself an education. There's a million things I want to know and books are full of 'em"

"If there's anything in particular that you want to know that I can help with, Cuthbert, then don't hesitate to ask."

Cuthbert nodded. " I notice that your Cooper is making a lot of wheels for carts. Why is that?"

"Well, we are now about to be come part of the pony express route to Montreal. Hudson's Bay Company have set up an office there. We expect there to be more carts on this route, and the roads are rough."

Cuthbert leaned back in his chair and patted his stomach.

"If I stay here much longer, I shall never be able to mount a horse again!" he laughed, then a cloud crossed his handsome face.

"But I keep forgetting that I have to go and take my medicine. I still believe in my principles, Peter. They haven't changed, except that I now know that there are men like you around who will give my people respect. I thank you for showing me that. And if I ever get the chance, I shall sign on with the Hudson's Bay Company"

Peter reached out and grasped his hand warmly.

"Thanks, Cuthbert. It doesn't change what's happened, but I understand it all"

Peter rode into the Selkirk settlement . The Summer sun shone warmly on his back and he looked around appreciatively at fields of healthy wheat, barley, potatoes.

"Hey, Fidler, Peter Fidler!"

The voice that hailed him was familiar. Colin Robertson!.

He put his horse to the trot and manoeuvred his way past playing children, carts, and a sewage ditch.

"Colin! What a surprise!" and he noticed the large group of Indians camped at the edge of nearby woods.

"Iroquois! I bet they are with you, Colin" he said, dismounting and offering his hand.

"They are indeed, Peter" smiled Robertson, slapping Fidler on the shoulder. "The world's greatest trappers. Well, present company excepted of course!. They'll show the Northwesters a thing or two. Come on in with me for a dram and I'll tell you more."

They moved off the roadway into the dim interior of an adjacent cabin. A bar ran the length of it. Robertson went behind and pulled out a stone jar of whisky.

"Did you see any of my Canadians along the route?" he asked as he poured to generous helpings into tin mugs.

"Can't say as I did, Colin, but I came from the Albany River and there wasn't a deal going on there. Where are they?"

"The other side of the colony. About a hundred of them. The Northwesters are building a new post on the original site of Fort Gibraltar. We'll keep an eye on them".

They clinked mugs and drank.

"Phew! Quite a bite!. Long time since I tasted proper whisky" gulped Peter.

"While you're getting your breath back, I can ask you if you'll help with the building of our new post, Halkett House.

And then there's a new Catholic Mission started at Red River under Father Provencher. Can I persuade you to attend mass there. I know you're Church of England, but your attendance will reassure certain people. All the Meurons and Canadians attend but none of the Scots."

"I see no reason why to avoid that, Colin. I'll attend tomorrow"

He wrote in his diary that he had 'attended Mass. The three Missionaries or priests are much beloved and indefatigable'.

Colin and he walked from the cabin to the fields where men and women were hard at work. They chatted about crops and weather until interrupted by the sound of a galloping horse. The rider dragged his horse to a standstill, flung himself off and in one movement had hitched it to a rail and gathered two leather pouches from its haunches.

"A canoe called about twenty minutes ago" said the rider with a strong accent. "Says these are important". He thrust the pouches into Robertson's hands.

"Let's sit on this log and have a quick look" said Colin.

One was a warrant for Peter Ogden, Fidler's enemy of some years ago. He was accused of murdering a Cree Indian at Green Lake three years previously.

There were others of a similar nature.

"I wonder if they ever give these things any serious practical consideration, Peter?. If we serve these now, and take the accused prisoner, we'll have to keep 'em for the winter. We don't have those facilities in space or guards. No. I'll think about it and serve them when the winter is over".

"The canoe has some other stuff for us, and York House has sent some cattle" said the rider.

"Cattle? What cattle? " asked Colin.

"2 cows, 1 bull, 2 sows, 1 boar and 22 hundredweights of bar iron. They travelling over country"

"I just hope they get here" commented Colin.

As Fidler and Robertson walked back into the settlement, Colin said "I would like to extend about twenty miles up river. Survey some lots at a place called Birsay, named after the Orkney home of Magnus Spence. Is it something you have time to do, Peter?. Although, I shan't be here when you get back".

Peter considered the proposal.

"I think I may be able to squeeze that in, Colin. I have been asked to survey Pembina and its relation to the 49th parallel which has been defined as the line separating British Territory from the United States. I'm not yet sure, but I have a feeling that the mission there, started by Father Dumoulin, will turn out to be in the United States"

A small party of Iroquois rode by and saluted Robertson gravely. He waved back .

They sat on the steps of another cabin. Inside, a woman sang to herself and the sound of a besom could be heard.

A man stooped to pass his height under the doorway, looked at the two seated men and took a position alongside Peter. He took off a battered bowler hat and wiped an arm across his forehead.

"A lovely day, Gentlemen" It sounded like ' shentlemen'.

"Good day Mr Sutherland" said Peter and Colin in unison.

"We are still losing horses to the Indians" observed Colin. "I'm going to send to the Mandans for a new supply. Is it something that you would wish to do Mr Sutherland?"

"I think it is something that can be done by me and my men" observed Sutherland. " But I won't buy horses that are poor or too expensive. I believe that Jack Spense is coming with five men and 100 horses, but I am doubtful if we shall see that many! I expect the greater part of them to be stolen before they reach the settlement"

They talked about horses and the future.

"We expect to have plenty of horses for spring ploughing but we don't have a Blacksmith. Can we borrow your Smith who seems to be the only one capable of making plough irons?"

Peter agreed to consult the Blacksmith. Light was fading, so the men made their way to their cabins.

Early in the morning, Robertson called on Fidler.

"Early bird" said Peter, tugging at his leather breeches.

"Have to move out, Peter. Couldn't go without saying farewell. I have about 200 men to guide northwards and meet William Williams, our new Governor in Chief. "

"That must have arrived in yesterdays mail" said Peter. "Isn't he the sea Captain? He has a reputation as a redoubtable fighter. "

"So I'm told, Peter, so I'm told. He may be the man we need to bring about the demise of the enemy. So I'll say goodbye again, and trust that providence will join our paths".

Colin and his small army left.

One year later, in 1819, Fidler heard with dismay that Robertson had been captured and nothing was reported about his army.

Peter and Mary walked hand in hand among the trees by the river.

Two small children romped and tugged at their legs.

"I think the older boys are beginning to spread their wings now, Mary. I had thought of sending them to England to finish their education in the way that our friends have done. I have taught them as much as I know about mathematics, reading, writing, surveying, astronomy over the years. What do you think?"

They stopped beneath a sweetly scented tree, alive with blossom and he placed an arm around her waist.

"I am not sure that England will suit them, husband. You have described many things to me and the boys but those things seem strange and foreign. Thomas is now twenty four and an interpreter, but I am ashamed to say that he has begun to fall into idleness with his Indian friends. He may be worse away from your influence in a strange place. "

Peter sighed. "At his age, there is little I can tell him or make him do or not do, Mary. I feel that I have failed somewhere. Even Charles at twenty one has begun to disobey me. He is a very good steersman, but his relationship with the wife of James Inkster is very bad."

"I know that you are very saddened, husband. I wish it could be different. But you must not blame yourself. Other influences are at work on people and the children must begin to make up their own minds about what is right and wrong. Whatever you do, I shall support you".

He looked into her eyes and serious face.

"Be happy, darling Mary" he said lovingly. "I have you and you have me. That should mean something".

He wrote in his annual report

'Charles Fidler, Steersman, behaved with great impropriety last spring'

'Thomas Fidler, Interpreter, Not fit for being an interpreter. Disobedient, careless of the property and afraid of the Indians but very hardy and ingenious'

He chewed at the feathers of his quill pen and wrote a heading 'Regional report for 1819'

Mary shooed the small children away from their father's knees , put a mug of steaming tea on the table and slipped out quietly on mocassin feet.

Peter was engrossed and nodded vaguely. He wrote that the barley crop had been almost entirely ravaged by grasshoppers and the dry summer drought of the previous two years had affected all vegetables including the potatoes which had been a staple diet in the region since 1780.

He changed tack and reported the techniques of sturgeon fishing and that manure is seldom used on the land.

He recorded that he would be travelling to Red River later and would arrange for the preparation of boats to go to York Factory and also for canoes to carry pemmican to Rainy Lake where they would meet the Montreal convoy.

He was aware that the Company was about to send a strong force into Athabasca.

The day of the Northwesters had passed and Hudson's Bay had taken the lead.

Then Robertson appeared as though by magic.

He told how he had escaped his captors. Peter was able to tell him that even during his absence, the Hudson's Bay trade had increased and the supply of furs was considerable.

"Did you hear of William Williams coup, Peter" said Robertson from the comfort of a soft chair.

"A bit of rumour, Colin, but only speculation"

"Well, he laid a trap for the convoy of Northwesters which passes down river towards Lake Winnipeg. The Masters normally travel in pairs and he netted seven major Northwesters, including Angus Shaw and J G McTavish!"

Peter whistled in surprise.

"That must have shaken them up" he said with enjoyment.

"Another piece of information which may please you is that your old enemies, Peter Skene Ogden and Samuel Bully Black have both volunteered to go as far away as possible out of the reach of the law. Good riddance, I say"

He felt around in his pockets, took out a knife and some hard tobacco which he began to pare some into the bowl of a short pipe.

"I'm going to move northwards again soon, Peter. Will you provide the provisions?"

Peter agreed unconditionally.

"I don't know whether you heard about our grasshoppers, Colin, but they devastated our crops for a long while. I have a feeling that they will return this year. I find that I'm much more interested in locally important issues these days rather than company politics.

"I understand that, Peter, with a certain amount of envy. I shall be glad to settle when the time comes".

He knocked the pipe embers into the fire.

"Incidentally, I understand that Mary is expecting again?"

"She is indeed" said Peter proudly ."Due in June. I was going to meet the Mandans and set up trade arrangements, but that will have to wait. I can write to MacKay at Brandon House to supply them with a little tobacco and to let them know that we shall be pleased to trade with them at the full moon in December"

Colin took out a leather pouch, placed the pipe inside it and pushed it into a side pocket. He stood and stretched his arms to the front and sighed.

"Things are certainly changing, Peter. It seems strange to have Cuthbert Grant on our side now, "

"Yes, and I'm very pleased. I grew to like him a lot. I understand that he will be made Master at Beaver Creek. It is something he wanted but never expected"

"Well, goodbye Peter. I hope that we'll meet again soon. I'll try to keep out of the Northwesters clutches!"

And he left.

There was a great deal of activity during the summer.

The whole Sioux nation turned up at the colony, made speeches of everlasting peace.

At the same time, 70 Stone Indians visited the Mandans on the Missouri and only 7 returned the remainder having died from smallpox or measles.

Mary's child was born in June and named Margaret. Her children Sally, Andrew, Alban and Polly all contracted measles.

So did Margaret, who died.

Peter talked with Mary about his future.

"I've been sent to take over Fort Dauphin in September, Mary. I think it should be a comfortable period of our life with our family, me with my books and where the tribe is friendly. What are your thoughts?"

She looked at him searchingly.

"You have not been well recently, my husband. I trust that the load will not be too great for you. Your strength has become less and you have difficulty walking. If you can overcome those things, then I think you will be alright. "

From November 3rd onwards, he became suddenly bed ridden, but recorded his symptoms. "I am still unable to leave my bed on 30th November 1819"

"December. I can get up for short periods".

"Some of our children are also ill. Andrew and Clement have been delirious and sick. Polly has stomach pains. Charles has been ill but seems better now"

Peter bounced back to his normal self in Spring and continued his gardening with enthusiasm. He recorded that much of his sickness had been in his head, but a report produced by him in 1820 showed no such signs.

Peter sat on the front step of their cabin, balancing a journal on his knees. Spring sunshine poured around him. The hum of bees was accompanied by the hum of children in the nearby school chanting their lesson.

Mary pulled up a rocking chair and sat with the youngest baby on her lap.

"There are a few things I'd like to add to this Report of the District, Mary" he said and wrote his heading "Report of the District 1820".

"I suppose they ought to be aware of its size, which I calculate as 25,960 square miles"

He sat in thought for a moment. Two horsemen cantered by. One raised his battered leather hat. Peter smiled and waved his pen.

"I suppose that means there must be an Indian for every twenty-five square miles! I think I'll include that"

He became engrossed in his work. Mary watched him closely, rocking and occasionally crooning to the sleeping child.

As new ideas occurred to him, he spoke aloud, briefly, then wrote. He included information about rivers and lakes and referred to the history of trading posts in the region. He commented about his principal customers, the "Bungee" people, whose name is believed to have derived from their use of the word 'bungee' meaning 'small' when referring to the measures that traders offered.

"I believe I'll comment about their origins in this area" he mused and wrote that they had been brought from the Rainy Lake and Lake Superior in 1797 by the North West Company and had settled in the region.

Having started he reported a wealth of ethnological detail about the native indians, their dress, habits, family and domestic practices, employ-ment, custom etc.

"I suppose that what they trade for must say something about them, Mary. For example, the Bungees and Saulteaux take payment in clothing, guns kettles, but the Cree take theirs in rum".

Mary, a Cree, rocked impassively.

He put away his journal and tools, stood and went to Mary's side.

"I shall be going away for a little while in May, probably until July" he said. "I have to report to York Factory. I'd like to get a message to Norman McCleod at Fort William. There are some books and papers I want returned which were taken in June 1816 when they looted Brandon House"

He turned into the doorway.

"I think that I'll rest a moment, Mary. Did I tell you that our new boss, Mr George Simpson will be at York? I may get to meet him. I understand that he has no Rupert's Land experience and has it all to learn. A difficult position in which to be".

There were many lights in the reception room of the large cabin.

The clothing was a mixture of modern European styles and practical local styles.

"I've hear a great deal about you, Mr Fidler. I think I am going to rely on your advice and guidance for a long time to come. May I call you Peter?"

George Simpson was a small elegant man who seemed genuinely pleased to be introduced to Peter.

"Thank you Mr Simpson.'ll do whatever is needed" replied Peter .

"The Company is doing well again, Peter, especially in the area of Lake

Athabasca, thanks to the efforts of Colin Robertson with support from you and your colleagues. Did you hear that he had been captured for a second time at Grand Rapids and transported to Montreal?"

Peter shook his head and was unable to hide his look of surprise.

"Yes. " Simpson continued "My latest information is that he has escaped for a second time also and gone to the United States for passage to England"

"The Northwesters have spent a lot of energy and money in trying to get rid of us, Mr Simpson. They haven't succeeded and my own view is that they will topple to disaster. Their partnership agreement ends in 1821 and there's no knowing what will happen"

"Quite so, Peter. I am aware that several partners are preparing to withdraw. One of them is Dr John McLoughlin who is not pleased with McGillivray's style of management"

He offered a box of cheroots to Peter who declined with thanks.

"Not everybody's taste" said Simpson."But enough of business and the Company. I have heard about your wife and family. Have you brought her with you?"

"I would normally try to do so, Mr Simpson, but she is expecting another child and remains at Norway House. I shall return there, at the end of my business here, then take them on to Fort Dauphin in August".

"Well, as much as I would like to stay and dally longer with you, Peter, I must make the rounds. It has been a pleasure meeting you and I hope we meet many times in the future."

They shook hands and parted.

George Simpson remained Head of the Company's operations for the next thirty years and retired with a Knighthood.

Peter travelled home in August and met his new son, Peter born on 9th July.

On the trail to Dauphin, his group met Colonel Dickinson.

"Well met, Peter" hollered Dickson from a hundred yards away and closing. "How the devil are you?"

They met in an open space and leaned from their horses to shake hands warmly.

"I'm fine, Colonel. And you look like a spring chicken!"

Dickson removed his hat and bowed gravely to Mary who smiled with pleasure.

They exchanged their intended destinations and Dickson said

"Have you heard about Lord Selkirk?"

"Nothing for quite a while" replied Peter.

"Yes. 'Fraid he died and so did Sir Alexander MacKenzie. There soon won't be many of us old timers left at this rate! Incidentally, I don't think you've met John Pritchard yet. He's an ex-Northwester who has the idea of setting up a company to provide Buffalo wool for weaving.. Everybody's talking about it at Dauphin, so you'll be ready for it! "

Peter's group continued their journey without incident. . The weather was fine and they were met by Peter's sons George and Thomas and a number of staff.

"Have you heard about the Buffalo wool, father" asked George excitedly, pumping Peter's arm.

"He's only just got here!" exclaimed Thomas jostling to grab Peter's hand.

"Heard all about it on the trail from a Night Owl. Mr Pritchard, isn't it?"

They stared at him, then burst into laughter.

"Of course!. Colonel Dickinson!" said George. "You'd have met him on the trail"

"You got me going for a minute, father. Night Owl indeed!" laughed Thomas, crossing to Mary and kissing her on both cheeks as she hugged him.

"Follow me, father, and I'll take you to your new quarters" said George, hugging Mary then picking up two bundles and leading the way.

A small crowd had gathered and numbers of men and women, Indians and Europeans greeted Peter and his party.

Peter put his arm around Mary's shoulders to guide her across the rutted street.

"Seems a peaceful place, Mary. I'm looking forward to a rest. How do you feel?"

"Happy to see my older sons again, husband. Happy that you feel fine".

That evening, by oil lamp, Peter updated his records.

Mary brought a flagon of mulled ale and sat quietly by his side.

He looked at her silently, then spoke.

"I need your approval, Mary. I have written up my records. These may be the last ones here before returning to Norway House. I would like to read them and listen to your thoughts. As you know, I am required to comment about my staff and that includes George and Thomas"

"Read " said Mary turning to face him.

Peter moved to get the best light on his records, cleared his throat and read.

"George Fidler, a Boatman. Has been friends with the Indians for seventeen years. Active. A Moose Hunter"

He looked up at Mary. She nodded but said nothing.

He continued.

"Thomas Fidler. A Writer. Very handy in the Carpenter way but rather addicted to liquor"

He sat and waited.

Mary too was silent, then she said.

"Your words about both of them are true, husband. I would have it no other way"

He leaned and kissed her. There was nothing for them to say. Their looks spoke all.

He wrote a final passage concerning the NorthWest Company.

"I believe they are now on their last legs".

He did not know, but at the time of his entry, an Amalgamation Agreement was being drawn up in London which brought an end to the North West Company of old. It became bankrupt in 1824 and Hudson's Bay Company monopolised trade in the British Territories of North America.

Winter passed tranquilly. Peter fished, indulged his passion for gardening and observation. Mary mingled with the women of her own and other tribes and gathered information. The children played, worked or went to school. The bad old days seemed impossible.

In the summer, they packed, said their goodbyes and left for Norway House.

The journey was uneventful until Nicholas Garry arrived from London with news of the amalgamation and ideas for reorganisation.

He talked at length with Peter and recorded the results.

Peter became ill again.

The weather permitted him to sit outside in the rocking chair, wrapped in a thick tartan blanket.

Nicholas arrived in the early afternoon and sat beside him, eating a savoury stew prepared by Mary.

"I was very sorry to hear of your illness, Peter. If there is anything that

I or the Company can do, then do not hesitate to ask. I understand that it was the palsy?"

Peter nodded. Speaking was difficult.

"You are of course still the District Master, Peter. If you wish, I can relieve you of that aspect of your work and arrange for you to be employed as a Geographer. There are a couple of other matters which are important to me that I would wish to discuss with you."

Nicholas put down his spoon, pushed the dish away and burped. Mary smiled with pleasure and signalled a further helping.

"I really couldn't Mrs Fidler. My poor horse will neve forgive me !"

"Where was I? Oh yes! Your maps at York Factory. I'd like to arrange for them to be sent to England. The world's map makers are biting their nails to get first hand information of the British Territories and your maps are incomparable. As a Geographer, you will remain in the service of course and have a retired share. You will remain the winter at Norway House with Mr Robertson to help you. Is that to your liking?"

Peter nodded. A hearty voice hailed from the corner of the building.

"Good day to you gentlemen and ladies"

The Reverend John West, recently arrived from the Red River colony and a friend of Nicholas Garry, stepped nimbly up the wooden steps. He looked down at boots muddied to the calf and pulled a face, then smiled.

 Peter held out a hand which West took.

"I think you look a lot better than you did yesterday, Peter. I called but you were sleeping. I understand you want me to do something for you"

"Yes" said Peter through the corner of his mouth. "Want marriage and want christenings"

"Good Heavens! Both at once? Of course not. I assume you mean marriage to your lady, Mary. "

He turned to Mary who was standing near the door. "I 'm right, aren't I Mary?"

Mary nodded, her face suffused with pleasure, her eyes filled with tears.

"As for the christenings, I'm not sure it makes a bit of difference whether that comes first or afterwards, but I'll check my diary"

He placed one long leg over the balustrade and dangled a muddied leather boot. His back was to a post supporting the verandah.

"Right, Mary. I can do both. The christenings I can fit in comfortably and with pleasure on 12th August."

He looked up.

"How many children?"

"Four, Chaplain" said Mary. "Mary, Clement, Colet and Peter"

"Fine. Fine" said John, making notes. "We'll work out the details later. Now, the wedding can take place the next day. No. No. Wait a minute. No. The day after that would be better, say 14th August. Will that be suitable?"

Peter and Mary nodded.

"With your permission, I would like to attend" said Nicholas Garry " and your old friend Donald Sutherland will be here by then. He will want to attend also"

The pleasure on Peter and Mary's faces was evident. Mary moved alongside him and took his hand.

The baptisms took place as scheduled. In the Register of Marriages for 14th August 1821 is recorded

"Peter Fidler of Manitobah and Mary, an Indian Woman of the same place, were married at Norway House on this Fourteenth day of August 1821 by me, John West, Chaplain".

It was signed by Peter Fidler and Mary made her mark in the presence of two witnesses, Nicholas Garry and Donald Sutherland

Some weeks later, he looked up to see a familiar face above him.

"By all that's holy! J G McTavish!"

His speech had improved and he had regained the use of his hands. He extended one to his old enemy.

"Sit down McTavish, sit down. Strangely I'm pleased to see you again"

"Aye, Peter. I could'na pass without seeing you. I'm right sorry that you have been unwell but I hear that you are improving"

"I hear that you've been appointed as the Chief Factor at York. I'm very happy for you. I have written to Nicholas Garry asking him to consider me in employment as an Indian Trader at any post when I get better. So, I may meet you on the trail again but under more friendly circumstances."

"Weel, laddie. It's not entirely social that I'm here. I have brought young Taylor with me. He's a good sketcher and I'd like to borrow one of your maps if I may, just to say that I have copied an original one, if you know what I mean!"

His shrewd face considered Peter. "If you'd like an important job until your health returns, laddie, I can have words with Garry and arrange for you to go as the Clerk at Fort Dauphin. You won't be required to produce a Regional Report but you'll retain your normal salary . I know that both you and Mary liked it there and it seems a good place to rest".

Peter looked at Mary. She smiled and nodded.

"Sounds fine to me, McTavish. Mary will fix us a drink and then we'll talk about the map,. Where is young Taylor?"

Later, whilst on his own, he drew up his Will. The Executives were to be the Governor in Chief of Hudson's Bay Company, the Governor of Lord Selkirk's Colony at Red River and Secretary of the Hudson's Bay Company.

He was transferred to Fort Dauphin for the winter of 1821/1822. He no longer was required to write reports but was written about as an employee.

Three entries were made.

"Annual Assessment. Peter Fidler. A faithful and interested old servant, now superannuated. Has had a recent paralytic affliction and his resolution quite gone. Unfit for change.

"Youngest child Harriet was born (to Peter & Mary Fidler) on 9th July."

"Cumberland House, 26th January 1822. We also learn that Mr Peter Fidler departed this life at Fort Dauphin on 17th of last month"

Finally, a mere four years later, on 26th June 1826, his wife, Mary Fidler, followed him and was laid to rest in the Red River settlement by the Reverend David T Jones, Chaplain of the Hudson's Bay Company.

Fort Dauphin, Manitoba, Canada

Cairn

To the mempry of Peter Fidler (1769-1822) of Bolsover, Derbyshire, England, Explorer and Surveyor for the Honourable Hudson's Bay Company.
Erected by the National Historical and Heritage Department, Manitoba, Canada.

CHAPTER 13

Finale - Conclusion & Fidler's Will

Back home, in Bolsover, Derbyshire, England there is no local hero.

Robin Hood may lurk around the Nottinghamshire corner, but he was not a Derbyshire man. It is unlikely that he was 'real' whereas Peter Fidler was.

It is a little over two hundred years ago at the time of writing this account in 1999 that Pete Fidler made his entrance on to the stage of English and Canadian events.

Fidlers of the same clan abound in Bolsover, descendants of Peter's father's family and of his brother Joseph.

Descendants of Mary and Peter Fidler abound in Canada, around the Bolsover Fort area of Meadow Lake, Lesser Slave Lake, Dawson Creek, Red River Settlement and many other places. Their numbers are estimated as being close to 11.000.

Metis, and blood-relatives of those in England.

English men and women can be proud of Peter Fidler originally of Bolsover, Derbyshire, England, who displayed all those qualities which for generations have been admired by the English.

Company records show that he was, stable, trustworthy, enduring, with a stubborn refusal to surrender, no matter the odds, how unequal the contest. He kept on fighting to the end, like a bulldog, as when he returned to face the viciousness and treachery of the North Westers.

He was a man of his word, of honour whose courage was quiet, without ostentation and as one writer has put it 'Without the dashing courage of the flashy Highlanders of the North West Company".

His activities showed great expertise as a Surveyor, Explorer, Geographer, Meteorologist, Adventurer, Ethnologist, Botanist, Astronomer, Recorder, Linguist.

During thirty three years he was a loyal, uncomplaining servant of his Company and Company Master at a number of far flung trading posts.

His own contribution to filling in the map of Canada was considerable. Others may have been first at places or travelled earlier, but he was among the first true cartographers to draw up maps and describe the geography of great areas of Alberta, Manitoba, Saskatchewan and prepare the way for Winnipeg, Calgary, Edmonton and other modern cities.

He had lived with and recorded the Plains Indians, the Woodland Indians, the Barren Ground Indians of various tribes, learned their languages and observed their customs.

From his first surveys in 1791 in canoe, on horseback, on foot, by sled and on snowshoes, an area 1300 miles east to west and 900 miles north to south, he covered 48,000miles.

Throughout the long journeys, he maintained not only maps, but notes and journals many of which are with us today. He left them to the Hudson's Bay Company so that his records of the very early West could be available to scholars of the future.

In one of his notebooks, details of his children were kept.

They read as follows :-

Thomas	June 20th	1795	York Factory
Charles	Oct 10th	1798	Cumberland House
George	Nov 10th	1800	Chesterfield House
Sally	Nov 26th	1802	Nottingham House
Decusroggan	Oct 12th	1804	Nottingham House
Died	Mar 8th	1814	
Andrew	Nov 29th	1806	Cumberland House
Alban	Jun 17th	1809	Holy Lake
Mary	June 27th	1811	Charlton Portage
Faith	Aug 26th	1813	Red River
Died	Oct 6th		1813 Brandon House
Clement	Nov 24th	1814	Brandon House
Colette	Mar 5th	1817	Halketts House
Margaret	May 12th	1819	Red River
Died	Jul 21st	1819	Red River Forks
Peter	Jul 2nd	1820	Norway House
Harriet	Jul 9th	1822	Norway House

Several of them married well, for example, Sally who became the partner of Governor William Williams.

In his Will, he provided for all his family. By standards of the day he was a fairly rich man.

An unusual bequest was left in clause 7 of the Will which reads as follows.

" All my money in the funds and other personal property after the youngest child has attained twenty-one years to be placed in the public funds and the interest annually due to be added to the capital and continue so until August 16th 1969 (I being born on that day two hundred years before) when the whole amount of the principal and interest so accumulated I Will and desire to be then placed at the disposal of the next male child heir in direct descent from my son, Peter Fidler"

This aspect of his Will was overturned by the Courts as being impractical and in 1827 his estate was passed to his eldest son Thomas as executor. The proceeds, divided among members of his family, gave them about 200 pounds each, a not inconsiderable sum at the time and very useful if used wisely. On the whole, it was not so used, it was wasted, and Peter's mathematical bequest evaporated.

Others have calculated that by 1969, whoever the recipient should have been, it would have matured in the region of 200 million pounds!

Acknowledgements and Bibliography

I wish to pay tribute to the following people and authorities for their enormous help, guidance and support for which a researcher and historian in this field must be sincerely grateful.

Mrs Mary Fidler of Bolsover, England and her great range of memorabilia including :- Details of Peter Fidler's Will, 'Hudson's Bay House' Building Costs. Parts of Peter Fidler's Journals, Peter Fidler's Father's Will. Information derived from regular contact with Peter Fidler's descendants in Canada. Numerous photographs.

References from **The Public Archives of Canada**, Ottawa. Material from **The Hudson's Bay Company's** records at **Manitobah Museum** with particular reference to the assistance and advice given by Archivists Debra Moore and Judith Beattie and their invaluable assistance with copyright matters of images from their unique collection.

Richard Glover's edition of David Thompson's 'Narrative .

J G MacGregor: "Peter Fidler: Canada's Forgotten Surveyor" which was of inestimable value for date sequencing.

Derbyshire County Library, Local Studies Section, Chesterfield, England together with

Bolsover District Council, Tourism and Leisure Department for access to researched but unpublished material.

Bolsover District Library, Bolsover, England,

Bolsover Civic Society, especially Brenda Pegge.

If I have missed anyone who should be included, I offer a sincere and complete apology and thank them for their invaluable information.

K. Gordon Jackson.
January 2000